AF449032

GENERAL ORDERS

SPAIN AND PORTUGAL

APRIL 27TH TO DECEMBER 28TH, 1809

VOLUME I.

A photographic reproduction of the original
edition printed in London, 1811, by T. Egerton.

2022
Waterville, Maine
pagesofpages.com

INTRODUCTION TO VOLUME ONE

The *General Orders* can be considered the beginning of the enormous amount of printed material that was produced to document the military career of the Arthur Wellesley, Duke of Wellington. Ten annual volumes were issued in all, ending with the volume for 1818, the end of the occupation of France by the allies.

This first volume begins with the reason for their publication.

> The Commander of the Forces has been pleased to direct that the standing General Orders for the Army under his command should be printed, not only for the more perfect reference to them as a Code of Regulations, which practice has established as essentially necessary for a British Army in the Field, but also to enable the Adjutant General to furnish immediately every Regiment that joins the Army, or every new Division or Brigade that may be formed, with complete Copies of all the Rules and Orders which have been issued from time to time, for the Conduct and Guidance of the British Forces serving in the Peninsula.

Several collections of the General Orders were printed in the half-century following the war. The most notable were the two editions by Lieut.-Colonel John Gurwood, the editor of the twelve volumes of Wellington's Dispatches; the first, published in 1832, covered though 1815, and the second, 1837, continued though 1818 and the occupation of France. Those editions were compilations of extracts from the original volumes, arranged by category, and omitting many materials – for example, the reports of general courts martial, so numerous in this first volume, are given only as representative samples, with the names of the offenders. and even of their regiments, redacted.

The complete list of the volumes of General Orders is given on the next page.

Vol	Pub Date	Contents	Title Variations
1	1811	April 27th - Dec 28th, 1809	General Orders. Spain and Portugal. Volume I. London: Printed by Authority by T. Egerton
2	1812	January 2nd to December 29th, 1810.	General Orders. Spain and Portugal. Volume II. London: Printed by Authority by T. Egerton
3	1811	January 1st to December 31st, 1811.	General Orders. Spain and Portugal. Volume II. London: Printed by Authority by T. Egerton
4	1813	January 1st to December 30th, 1812.	General Orders. Spain and Portugal. Volume IV. London: Printed by Authority by T. Egerton
5	1814	January 7th to December 28th, 1813.	General Orders. Spain and France. Volume V. London: Printed by Authority by T. Egerton
6	1817	1814	General Orders. France, 1814. Volume VI. to which is added a general alphabetical index for the orders of 1809, 1810, 1811 & 1812. London.
7	1815	April 11 to December 31st, 1815.	General Orders. Flanders and France. Volume VII. Paris: Military Press.
8	186?	1816	General Orders. France, 1816. Volume VIII. Cambrai.
9	1816	1817	General Orders. France, 1817. Volume IX. 206 p. [Cambrai.] Printed at the Head Quarters of the Army [by Serjeant Buchan 3rd. Foot Guards]1817.
10	1816	1818	General Orders. France, 1818. Volume X. Cambrai.

GENERAL ORDERS.

SPAIN AND PORTUGAL.

APRIL 27TH TO DECEMBER 28TH,

1809.

VOL. I.

LONDON.

Printed by Authority,

BY T. EGERTON, MILITARY LIBRARY, WHITEHALL.

1811.

(iii)

HEAD QUARTERS.
14th Nov. 1810.

THE Commander of the Forces has been pleased to direct that the standing General Orders for the Army under his command should be printed, not only for the more perfect reference to them as a Code of Regulations, which practice has established as essentially necessary for a British Army in the Field, but also to enable the Adjutant General to furnish immediately every Regiment that joins the Army, or every new Division or Brigade that may be formed, with complete Copies of all the Rules and Orders which have been issued from time to time, for the Conduct and Guidance of the British Forces serving in the Peninsula.

By Order of His Excellency
The Rt. Hon. Visc. WELLINGTON, K. B.
Commander of the Forces.

CHARLES STEWART, M. Gen.
Adjutant General

NOTE.

THE General Orders of the Army have invariably been issued by paragraphs, each being numbered for the more easy reference to any particular point of the General Orders of the day.

It is to be observed, however, that in order to make the printed Volumes as concise as possible, all paragraphs are omitted which relate only to temporary regulation or incidental circumstances. But it has been found expedient in the Edition to make no change of the Numbers, in consequence of the omission of any paragraphs, as there are references throughout the General Orders to the numbers of the paragraphs as they at present stand.

N. B. Where there is a lapse of Dates, on those days no General Orders of moment have been issued.

G. O.

1. HIS Majesty has been pleased to appoint Lieutenant General Sir Arthur Wellesley, K. B. to be Commander of his Forces in Portugal, and His Excellency having arrived in this country to assume the command, all reports, applications, &c., are henceforward to be addressed to him through the usual channels.

His Excellency having appointed the following Officers to be his Aides de Camps, they are to be obeyed accordingly.

Lieut. Col. Bathurst, 60th Foot, Military Secretary. . . . .
Captain The Hon. Fitzroy Stanhope, 1st Gds.
————— Lord Fitzroy Somerset, 43 F. . .
————— Henry Bouverie, Coldst. Gds. . .
————— George Canning, 3 Gds. . . . . .

} Aides de Camp.

Staff of the Forces in Portugal.

Lieut. General Sir Arthur Wellesley, K. B.
Commander of the Forces.

Major Gen. Sherbrooke . .
—————— Payne . . .
—————— Lord W. Bentinck
—————— Paget . .

} With the local rank of Lieut. Generals in Portugal . during the continuance of this service.

Major General Cotton
—————— Hill .

Major General Murray
———————— Erskine
———————— M'Kenzie
———————— Tilson
Brigadier General A. Campbell
———————— H. Campbell
———————— R. Stewart
———————— A. Cameron
———————— H. Fane
———————— Drieberg
———————— Langworth
Colonel Donkin, Colonel on the Staff

Adjutant General's Department.

Brigadier Gen. The Hon. Charles Stewart, Adjutant Gen.

Lieut. Col. Darrock, 36th Regiment .
———————— Lord Aylmer, Coldst. Gds. .
Bt. Lt. Col. Hinuber, 68th Foot . . } Assistant
Lt. Col. John Elley, R. Regt. Horse Gds. } Adjutant
Major F. S. Tidy, 14th Foot . . . . } Generals.
Bt. Major Williamson, 30th do. . . .
Major Geo. Berkeley, 35th do.. . . .
Major Colin Campbell, 70th do. . . .

Captain Willoughby Cotton, 3d Gds. .
———————— John Elliott, 48th Foot . . . } Deputy
———————— Charles Dashwood, 3d Gds. . } Assistant
———————— Francis Cockburn, 60th Foot . } Adjutant
———————— Vernon Graham, 26th do. . . } Generals.
———————— Henry Mellish, 87th do. . .

Lieut. George During, 1st Batt. K. G. L. is attached to this
Department until further orders.

Quarter

Quarter-Master General's Department.

Colonel George Murray, 3d Guards, Qr. Master General.
Lieut. Colonel Wm. Delancey, Perm. Staff

—————— James Bathurst, 60th Foot

—————— R. Bourke, Perm. Staff .

Major George Blaquiere, do. . . . .

—————— Augustus Northey, do. . . .

} Assistant Qr. Master Generals

Captain Matthew Sutton, 97th Foot .

—————— Algernon Langton, 61st do. .

—————— Dawson Kelly, 27th do. . . .

—————— J. Haverfield, 48th do. . . .

—————— George Scovell, 57th do. . . .

—————— Robert Waller, 103d do. . .

—————— William Beresford, 8 Gn. Bn. . .

} Deputy Assistant Qr. Master General.

Medical Department.

A. Thompson, Inspector of Hospitals.
— Bolton, Deputy Inspector of Hospitals.
C. Larchin . . . .
E. Somers . . . .
— Buchan . . . .

} Physicians.

I. F. Nicholay . . . .
—— Morrel . . . .
I. Forbes . . . .
L. Kraziesur . . . .
A. Bole . . . .
S. Higgins . . . .
H. Irwin . . . .
T. Cooke . . . .

} Staff Surgeons.

William

William Williams . . . . } Apothe-
William Graham . . . . } caries.

R. Mathews, Acting Apothecary.
W. H. O'Reily, Deputy Purveyor.
24 Hospital Mates.

Commissariat Department.

John Murray, Esq. Commissary General.
Cha. Dalrymple, Deputy Commissary General.
Rawlings . . . . } Act. Dep.
Boys . . . . } Commiss.
Dunmore . . . . } General.
Honeyman . . . .
O'Meara . . . .
Pratt . . . .
Murray . . . .
Gauntlett . . . . } Assistant
Young . . . . } Commissary
Dillon . . . .
Grieve . . . .
Aylmer . . . .
M'Kenzie . . . .
Coffin . . . .
Hodges . . . .
Pelken . . . .
Belson . . . . } Acting
Nelson . . . . } Assistant
Joly . . . . } Commissary
De Bels . . . .
Ogilvie . . . .
Downie . . . .

Haines

Haines . . . .
M'Donnell . . . .
Smidchin . . . .
Moore . . . .
Strahan . . . .
Haden . . . .
Melville . . . .
Dick . . . . . . , ...
Gordon . . . .
Brooke . . . .
Maude . . . .

} Acting Assistant Commissary.

Returns for 200 days bât and forage money, to be given in to the Quarter Master General, from the Generals, Staff Officers, and Regiments, lately landed in this country. Lieutenant General Payne, commanding the cavalry, will, on application to the Quarter Master General, have a Depôt Transport, placed at the disposal of the two regiments of cavalry last landed, to receive their stores, or such things as it is not expedient to land. The Lieutenant General may, if he shall think fit, leave the bayonets of the cavalry in store.

———————

ADJUTANT GENERAL'S OFFICE.
Pombal, 1st May, 1809.

G. O.

1. The 3d Dragoons, and 4th Dragoons, and the 2d Battalion, 24th Regiment, are to be under the orders of Major General M'Kenzie, sending their usual Returns to Head Quarters according to the General Orders.

2. Deputy Commissary Dalrymple is to be transferred,

B 3

from

from the Department of Accompts, to the Department of Stores.

3. General Officers to send in to the Adjutant General's Office at Head Quarters, as soon as possible, the names of the Officers composing their Staff.

4. A Return of all Orderlies, from the Cavalry Regiments, to be sent in, specifying to whom attached.

G. O.

ADJUTANT GENERAL'S OFFICE.
Coimbra, 3d May, 1809.

1. Returns to be sent, by the General Officers, and other individuals, entitled to Bât Men, and by the Commanding Officers of Corps, stating the number of Natives of Portugal, that have been hired, to serve in lieu of Bât Men, given by each Corps, and of the names of the several Officers, in whose service they are employed.

2. Upon all occasions, when the army will march, it will be in one or more columns, on one or different roads, with a view to take up a position, or by separate battalions, brigades, or larger divisions, with a view to occupy certain cantonments. In the first case, the reserve artillery and stores, drawn, or carried by horses or mules, are to follow the troops; then the baggage of regiments, and individuals of each column, is to follow, arranged in the order in which the corps or individual will stand in the column; and lastly, the artillery and commissariat stores on carts, drawn by bullocks.

3. In the other cases, when battalions or larger divisions are to take up cantonments, the baggage of each division, going to a separate cantonment, is to follow that division, and

and is to be arranged in the order, in which each corps or individual will stand in the order of march of the division, to which he may belong.

4. On all occasions, the leaders of columns, whether composed of the whole army, or of smaller divisions, will halt, once in every hour and a half, for five minutes, to allow the men to fall out; and Commanding Officers of companies will be held responsible if any man falls out of the ranks at any time during the march, excepting during these halts, or is absent from his company, at the end of it, upon any occasion, excepting sick and consequent inability to keep up.

5. If any man should be taken ill on a march, measures are to be taken for the care of him, according to the mode heretofore pointed out in the General Orders, particularly paragraph No. 11, of the General Order 24th April; and the Commanding Officer of his company will send a Non-commissioned Officer with him to the nearest magistrate as therein pointed out.

6. When circumstances will oblige battalions, in rear of any column, to halt, the head of such column must not be halted without the special orders of the Officer commanding the column, who will judge of the necessity of halting, according to the length of the interval which will thereby be occasioned in his column, the necessity there is that the column should be well closed up, and the probability that from the nature of the impediments of the road, the head of the column will soon be halted, and give time to the rear to close up.

7. Two Assistant Provosts, in addition to those already appointed, are to be appointed; and Commanding Officers of regiments and brigades will recommend such Non-

commissioned

commissioned Officers as they may think trust worthy and capable of performing the duties which will be required from them; they will receive Ensign's pay and allowances.

8. Depôts are to be established at the following places, upon which subject the Commissary General will receive directions, viz.

Rio Mayor, Leiria, Coimbra.—An Officer and 20 men of the 30th Regiment are to be stationed at Rio Mayor, and conduct the details of the duties there; the Senior Officer, in charge of the sick and convalescents at Leiria, is to conduct them at Leiria; and an Officer will be established at Coimbra, for the same purpose.

9. These Officers will correspond constantly with each other, and with the Quarter-master General of the army and Town Major at Lisbon.

10. Whenever stores or provisions are dispatched from Lisbon, the Quarter-master General is to be informed thereof, of the number of waggons or other means of conveyance on which they are laden, and of the route which they are directed to take, specifying by what stages. The Town Major is likewise to give notice of this dispatch to the Officer at Rio Mayor; this Officer is to relieve the escort, and send it back to Lisbon, and is to report the arrival and the probable departure of the convoy to the Quarter-master General and the Officer commanding at the next station; the Officers stationed at Leiria and Coimbra are to do the same respectively.

11. Non-commissioned Officers in charge of convoys will be held responsible for the conduct of the soldiers under their command on the march with convoys, and returning to their cantonments.

12. Captain

12. Captain Cooke of the Coldstream Guards is appointed a Deputy Assistant Adjutant General until his Majesty's pleasure is known.

13. His Majesty has been pleased to appoint Colonel Howorth of the Royal Artillery to be a Brigadier General on the Staff of the Army in Portugal.

14. Returns to be forthwith sent in to the Quartermaster General, of all carts or cars in use with corps, for what purpose required, where got, and by what authority.

15. A small sum of money being arrived, Paymasters of regiments will receive a sum of money on account of the estimates, from the 25th of April to 24th May, on application at the office of the Deputy Paymaster General.

16. Brevet Major Williamson, Assistant Adjutant General, is attached to the corps under the command of Major General Mackenzie, until further orders.

17. Captains Sutton and Langton, of the Quarter-Master General's Department, are likewise attached to the same corps until further orders.

18. General Orders will be issued, at the Adjutant General's Office, at 10 o'clock precisely, every morning. The Officers in the Department and Majors of Brigade to be responsible that the Adjutants have them by twelve.

ADJUTANT GENERAL'S OFFICE.

G. O.   *Coimbra, 4th May,* 1809.

1. The army will be brigaded, and stand in line, as follows, until further orders:

CAVALRY.

CAVALRY.

14th . . . .
20th . . . .
3d Light Dragoons K. G. Legion,
16th . . . . } Major General Cotton.

Coldstream Guards, 1st Battalion,
3d Ditto . . . . 1st Ditto .
1 Company 5th Bat. 60th Reg. } Brigadier General F. Campbell.

1st Brigade.

3d, or Buffs . . . .
66th . . . .
48th . . . .
1 Company 5th Bat. 60th Reg. } Major General Hill.

3d Brigade.

5 Companies 5th Bat. 60th Reg.
88th . . . .
1st Bat. Portuguese Grenadiers,
87th . . . . } Major General Tilson.

5th Brigade.

7th . . . .
1st Bat. 10th Portuguese Reg.
53d . . . .
1 Company 5th Bat. 60th Reg. } Brigadier General A. Campbell.

7th Brigade.

9th . . . .
2d Bat. 10th Portuguese Reg.
83d . . . .
1 Company 5th Bat. 60th Reg. } Brigadier General Cameron.

6th Brigade.

1st Battalion Detachments . .
1st Ditto 16th Portuguese Reg.
29th . . . . } Brigadier General R. Stewart.

4th Brigade.

2d Battalion Detachments . .
2d Ditto 16th Portuguese Reg.
97th . . . .
1 Company 5th Bat. 60th Reg. } Brigadier General Sontag.

2d Brigade.

27th Regiment . . . . . .
45th . . . .
31st . . . . } Major General M'Kenzie.

King's German Legion . . .
Brigadier General Langthwert .
———————— Drieberg . . } Major General Murray.

2. Although this is to be the order of the line of battle, circumstances of ground and situation may render a deviation from it necessary.

3. The light infantry companies belonging to, and the riflemen attached to each brigade of infantry, are to be formed together, on the left of the brigade, under the command of a Field Officer or Captain of light infantry of the brigade, to be fixed upon by the Officer who commands it. Upon all occasions, in which the brigade may be formed in line, or in column, when the brigade will be formed, for the purpose of opposing an enemy, the light infantry companies and riflemen will be of course in the

front,

front, flanks, or rear, according to the circumstances of the ground, and the nature of the operation to be performed. On all other occasions, the light infantry companies are to be considered as attached to their battalions, with which they are to be quartered or encamped, and solely under the command of the Commanding Officer of the battalion to which they belong.

4. An Assistant Commissary, with the necessary number of clerks, will be attached to each brigade of infantry, to each regiment of cavalry, to the artillery, and to head-quarters, to whom application must be made for provisions and supplies of all kinds required for the brigade, corps, or department, to which he will be attached. No requisitions must be made upon the country, excepting by the Commissary General, or his Deputy or Assistants, excepting in cases of necessity, in which small bodies of troops may be in upon their march, unattended by a Commissary, which case of necessity must always be clearly made out to the satisfaction of the Commander of the Forces.

5. All requisitions made contrary to this order, will be paid for by the Commissary, and the amount charged to the account of the Officer who will have signed it.

6. The Officers of the army must have observed the scarcity of all the supplies, which our army requires in Portugal; at the same time that the discipline and efficiency of the troops depend upon their regular delivery. The Commander of the Forces trusts, therefore, the General Officers of the army, and the Commanding Officers of regiments, particularly those who may be detached, will communicate constantly with the Officer of the Commissariat Department attached to their brigades and regiments,

ments, and will advise and assist them as far as may be in their power in their endeavouring to procure supplies for the troops.

7. One squadron, 14th Light Dragoons, 3d Light Dragoons, King's German Legion, and Major General Tilson's brigade of Infantry, will march to-morrow morning under the orders of Marshal Beresford. Major General Tilson will receive the orders for his march from Marshal Beresford.

8. The pay of the Officers who have been transferred to the Portuguese service, must be paid by the Paymaster of the regiment to which they belong, till it will have been notified in the Gazette, or in General Orders, that his Majesty has approved of their promotion.

9. Major Campbell, Assistant Adjutant General, is appointed to act as Commandant of Head-Quarters until further orders. Major Campbell will regulate all matters, concerning the quartering, marches, and police of head-quarters. Whenever the head-quarters are to move, all persons concerned are to send an Officer to the Commandant, for instructions relative to the moving of their baggage, &c. and for which a proper guard will be allotted by the Adjutant General.

Officers belonging to head-quarters will give strict injunctions to their servants in charge of their baggage, to have it ready at the place and time that shall be fixed by the Commandant; and they must be warned that all orders issued by him are to be implicitly obeyed, as he is answerable to the Commander of the Forces for the regular march of the baggage of head-quarters, and conduct of those who accompany it.

10. The appointment of the Staff of the Army in Portugal,

tugal, as detailed in the Orders of the 27th April, will bear date from the 1st April.

11. Major General Tilson's brigade, and the squadron 14th Light Dragoons, and 3d Light Dragoons King's German Legion, which will march to-morrow, are this day to receive three days bread and forage, for the 5th, 6th, and 7th instant.

12. The Commissary General will attach an Assistant Commissary, Clerks, &c. to the squadron 14th Dragoons and Hussars, which are to march to-morrow. The horses and mules belonging to the Officers of the Staff and regiments of infantry, are to receive forage from the Commissary only from day to day, unless any particular Officer should undertake to carry forward his forage, in which case forage will be delivered to him on the usual days of delivery.

13. Brigade's Sick Returns to be sent weekly, on Sunday morning, and monthly, on the 20th of every month, to the Head of the Medical Department of the Army, by the Staff Surgeons attached to brigades; and in the absence of the Staff Surgeon, all his duties, as directed in General Orders, are to be performed by the Senior Medical Officer, of whatever rank.

14. Serjeant Andrew Creagh of the 29th regiment, is appointed an Assistant Provost from the 4th instant.

G. O.

ADJUTANT GENERAL'S OFFICE.
Coimbra, 5th May, 1809.

1. The Hon. Lieutenant Colonel Cadogan, 2d battalion of the 71st Regiment, being with the army, by permission of the Commander of the Forces, and Captain

tain Burgh, 92d Foot, Aide-de-Camp to Sir John Craddock, are appointed extra Aides-de-Camp to His Excellency Lieutenant General Sir Arthur Wellesley.

2. Whenever an order is given for the troops to march on the following day, the Commissaries attached to those troops are to issue to them, one day's meat, which is to be cooked on that night, for the following day, so that the troops on their arrival at their new ground, having carried their provisions for the day, will be sure to have them.

3. The Officers belonging to the Royal Engineers Corps, will be attached to the army, as follows, till further orders.

Lieut. Boothby to the Brigade of Guards.
Lieut. Hamilton - - King's German Legion.
Lieut. Williams - - Major Gen. Hill's Brigade.
Lieut. Stanway - - Major Gen. M'Kenzie's Brigade.
Lieut. Jones - - - - Major Gen. Tilson's Brigade.

4. Lieutenant Colonel William Delancey, Permanent Assistant Quarter-Master General, to be Deputy Quarter-Master General to the Forces serving in Portugal, to bear date from the 1st of April; Captain James Henry Reynett, of the 52d regiment, to be Deputy Assistant Quarter-Master General, and to bear date from the 1st of April.

5. John Simpson, Serjeant in the 2d Battalion of the Line, King's German Legion, is appointed an Assistant Provost Marshal to the Army, bearing date from the 5th instant.

9. Serjeant Richard Webb, of the 3d Guards, is appointed

ed to act as Post-master with the army in the field, from the 24th April.

11. The Assistant Provosts are to receive each eighteen pounds, to purchase a horse, for which they are to draw forage.

12. Those horses of the Dragoons and Artillery, which will eat the corn and forage of the country, are to feed with that description of forage only; the Commanding Officers of Dragoons and Artillery will give directions that all their horses may be accustomed to the corn and forage of the country, by being fed at first, in the proportions of half English and half Portuguese corn and forage; then of two-thirds Portuguese and one-third English; and lastly of the whole Portuguese; the Commissary General will make his issues accordingly, to Cavalry and Artillery.

13. The Commander of the Forces calls the attention of the General, Field, and Staff Officers, to the foregoing order: it is very desirable that all horses should feed upon the forage of the country; and it is certain, that none will, unless they should by degrees be accustomed to it; he therefore recommends, that all the horses of the army should be fed in the proportions above directed for those of the Dragoons and Artillery. The Commissary General will be pleased to attend to the requisition of any General, Field, or Staff Officers, who may require a larger proportion of English forage for any particular horse, as far as his stores will allow.

ADJUTANT GENERAL's OFFICE.
Coimbra, 6th May, 1809.

G. O.

1. His Majesty has been pleased to appoint Brigadier General Sontag to the Staff of the Army serving in Portugal.

2. William Ferguson, Esq. Deputy Inspector of Hospitals, is to have charge of the Medical Department in the Field until further orders.

3. Captain Maw, Assistant Deputy Quarter-Master General, is attached to the Department until further orders.

4. Major General Cotton's, Major General Hill's, Brigadier General Stewart's brigades, and the King's German Legion will march to-morrow morning, at such hours, and by such routes as the Quarter-Master General will point out to the brigades respectively.

5. A six-pounder brigade of Artillery will march with the cavalry, half a light six-pounder brigade, with Brigadier General Stewart's brigade, and half a six-pounder brigade, with the King's German Legion.

6. The troops that are to march will receive, this day, bread and forage for three days, to the 9th instant, inclusive, and one day's meat to be cooked this day, for to-morrow.

7. The Commissary General will take care the Assistant Commissaries, attached to brigades of Infantry and regiments of Cavalry, have with them, each three days bread and three days meat for the troops to which they are attached respectively.

8. A squadron of Portuguese Cavalry, in Coimbra, is attached to Major General Cotton's brigade.

9. The Portuguese troops attached to the British brigades, are to be victualled by the Assistant Commissary of brigades to which they are attached, and are to receive each man, one pound and a half of bread, or one pound of biscuit, and half a pound of meat per diem. Cavalry the same as the British Cavalry.

10. Lieutenant General Payne is to command the British Cavalry in Portugal.

11. The Commander of the Forces recommends the Companies of the 5th Battalion of the 60th Regiment, to the particular care and attention of the General Officers commanding the brigades of Infantry, to which they are attached; they will find them to be most useful, active, and brave troops in the field, and that they will add essentially to the strength of their brigades.

Major Davy will continue to superintend the œconomy and discipline of the whole Battalion, and for this purpose will remain with that part of the army which will be most convenient to him, with a view of that object.

12. The Officers commanding brigades to which Portuguese troops are attached, will be allowed each to have an Interpreter, who will receive Ensign's pay and allowances; this person will likewise be allowed to draw forage for a horse.

13. The Serjeant Postmaster at head quarters, will be allowed 2s. per day, from the date of his acting as such.

14. Returns of the Interpreters allowed to General Officers commanding brigades, to which Portuguese battalions are attached, to be forthwith sent to the Adjutant General's office.

15. A. Thompson, Inspector of Hospitals, will remain

main in charge of the Medical Department at Lisbon, until further orders.

The Regimental Surgeons of the brigades, about to march, will immediately report the number of sick they intend to leave behind to Staff Surgeon Morrell, charged with the duty of superintending them. An Assistant Surgeon from each regiment will remain with the sick, till they are properly given over, and one or more Assistant Surgeons per brigade, according to the numbers, will remain in Coimbra to take care of them.

Subsistence to the 24th instant, at the rate of 10d. per day, for every man, must also be left in the hands of the Brigade Assistant Surgeon.

ADJUTANT GENERAL's OFFICE.
Coimbra, 7th May, 1809.

G. O.

1. BRIGADIER General Fane will assume the command of the Heavy Brigade of Cavalry, consisting of the 3d Dragoon Guards, and the 4th Dragoons

2. Mr. J. H. Cussin and Cypien Lasset Audrade, are attached to the Quarter-Master General's Department; the former with the pay and allowances of a Lieutenant of Cavalry, the other with the pay and allowances of a Cornet: appointments to bear date the 25th April.

3. Ensign Morgenthaul is continued as attached to the Quarter-Master General's Department until further orders.

4. The Commanding Officers of regiments will make reports to the Officers commanding brigades, at the moment they find any ammunition, of any man in the regiment they command, damaged or deficient, in order that requisition may be forthwith made to replace it, and that

the

the requisitions may not be made out at a moment a corps is to march.

5. The Commander of the Forces concludes that the ammunition of every Soldier in the army is inspected every parade.

6. Captain Holmes, of the 3d Dragoon Guards, is appointed Brigade Major to the Heavy Brigade of Cavalry, from the 25th ult.

Captain Robert Mercer, of the 3d Foot Guards, is appointed a Deputy Assistant Quarter-Master General, to bear date from this day.

———

ADJUTANT GENERAL'S OFFICE.
Coimbra, 8th May, 1809.

G. O.

1. THE brigade of Guards, Brigadier General A. Campbell's, Brigadier General Sontag's, a heavy and light six-pounder brigade, and Brigadier General Cameron's brigade, will march to-morrow morning, at the hours, and according to the routes, which will be sent to them by the Quarter-Master General.

2. Lieutenant General Sherbrooke will be so kind as to take the command of the three former, and Brigadier General Cameron will receive orders respecting the latter.

3. The troops which will march are this day to receive meat for to-morrow, which must be cooked, and three days bread and forage, for the 9th, 10th, and 11th instant inclusive.

4. The Commissary General will take measures that the Assistant Commissaries, with brigades, may besides be provided

vided with three days bread and meat, according to the directions he has received.

5. The head quarters will be fixed to-morrow, at the Quinta de Graciosa, on the right of the road beyond Pio.

6. The baggage of head quarters will move in rear of the troops, Officers belonging to it will receive instructions from the Commandant.

7. The sick of the brigades about to move, are to be deposited, this evening, at 5 o'clock, in the San Benito Convent, under the care of Staff-Surgeon Morrell, who will be there to receive them. The general orders of the 6th instant, and every part of all former orders relative thereto, are to be most strictly observed on the present occasion.

8. Returns of the number of sick left behind in each brigade, to be sent in as soon as possible.

9. A letter from the Commander in Chief, to Lieutenant General Sir Arthur Wellesley, Commander of the Forces in Portugal.

Horse Guards, 18*th April*, 1809.

SIR,

HAVING laid before the King the proceedings of a General Court Martial held at Lisbon, on the 21st February, 1809, and continued by adjournments to the 24th of the same month, for the trial of Ensign Robert Carter, of the 97th or Queen's own Regiment, who was arraigned under the undermentioned charges, viz.

1st Charge. For conduct highly unbecoming the character of an Officer and a gentleman, in drawing his sword upon a Portuguese inhabitant of Oporto, striking and ill-using him, upon the night of the 24th November, 1808, thereby creating a riot in the street, and tending to destroy

c 3

the

the harmony between the British and the Portuguese, so strongly inculcated to be preserved by the general orders in this country, in direct violation of his duty as an Officer, and to the prejudice of good order and military discipline.

2d Charge. For a gross violation of his duty as an Officer, in sending for a part of the regimental guard of the 97th Regiment, for the purpose of dispersing a guard of Portuguese troops, which had come to the spot in consequence of the tumult excited by Ensign Carter, thereby endangering the public peace of the town of Oporto, being a flagrant breach of discipline, and a direct violation of the Articles of War.

3d Charge. For making use of disrespectful, insolent, and threatening language, towards Captain Scott of the 45th Regiment, his superior Officer, on the night of the 24th November, being conduct highly unbecoming the character of an Officer and a gentleman, and a direct breach of the Articles of War.

4th Charge. For insubordination and disobedience of orders of Captain Scott, when Captain of the Piquet on the night of the 24th November, 1808, in refusing to give up his sword, rendering it in consequence necessary for the Portuguese Guard to take it away by force, and conveying him to their guard-house, thereby placing himself in a situation highly degrading to a British Officer, being a gross violation of military discipline, and a direct breach of the Articles of War.

Upon which charges the Court came to the following decision.

The Court having maturely weighed and considered, both for and against the prisoner, Ensign Robert Carter, of the 97th or Queen's own Regiment, and what he has

urged

urged in his defence, are of opinion that he is guilty of the first, second, and third charges, and likewise that he is guilty of the following part of the fourth charge, viz. insubordination, and disobedience of orders of Captain Scott, when Captain of the Piquet on the night of the 24th November, 1808, in refusing to give up his sword, it being a breach of the Articles of War, and do therefore sentence him, the said Ensign Robert Carter, of the 97th, or Queen's Own Regiment, to be cashiered. The Court do not find the prisoner guilty of the following part of the fourth charge, viz. rendering it necessary to take it, (the sword,) away by force, it appearing by the evidence, it was taken away from the prisoner, previous to the arrival of the Portuguese guard.

I am to acquaint you, that his Majesty was pleased to approve, and confirm the sentence of the Court. You will therefore acquaint me with the day upon which the sentence is made known to the prisoner, Ensign Robert Carter, as from that day, he will cease to receive pay in his Majesty's service.

I have the honour to be, &c.

(Signed)   DAVID DUNDAS,
Commander in Chief.

10. The Commanding Officer of the 97th Regiment will make known the Sentence of this General Court Martial to Ensign Robert Carter, and report the day of his having done so to this Office.

11. Purveyors Clerks are to receive each an allow-

ance

ance of 18l. to purchase a horse, for which they are to draw forage.

12. The Pay-master General will issue 400 dollars to the Senior Medical Officer, left in charge of the sick in Coimbra, over and above the 10d. per man, per diem, to be left with each patient, till the 24th inst. by the Pay-masters of Regiments.

13. Lieutenant Colonel Lord Aylmer, Assistant Adjutant General, is attached to Lieutenant General Sherbrooke, until further orders.

ADJUTANT GENERAL's OFFICE.
Coimbra, 8th May, 1809.

A. G. O.

1. LIEUTENANT General Paget being arrived to day, the Army is to be divided as follows, till the other Lieutenant Generals attached to it will join.

Guards . . . .
Major General Hill's . . . .
Brigadier General A. Campbell's
Brigadier General Cameron's . . } Right wing.

with a brigade of heavy 6 pounders, and a brigade of light 6 pounders . . . .
2. The King's German Legion . .
Brigadier General Sontag's . . .
Brigadier General R. Stewart's . . } Left wing.

with one brigade of six pounders, and one brigade of three pounders.

3. These

3. These wings will be formed into two or more lines, as circumstances may require, and brigades will be detached from them according to circumstances, to form advanced guards and reserves: there is to be no alteration in the orders of march to-morrow.

4. The brigade of Guards will leave an Officer in charge of their sick at Coimbra : one Officer of Brigadier General Cameron's brigade will be left to take charge of the sick of that brigade, and also the sick of Brigadier General Sontag's brigade ; one Officer of Brigadier General A. Campbell's brigade, will be left to take charge of the sick of it.

The Royal Artillery and Engineers.

Lieutenant Colonel Henuber, Assistant Adjutant General, is attached to the troops under the orders of Lieutenant General Honourable E. Paget ; and Captain Cotton, Deputy Assistant Adjutant General to the Cavalry under Lieutenant General Payne.

Memorandum.—Orders will always be given out immediately on the arrival of Head Quarters at a New Station ; Brigade Majors will come provided with the addresses of their General Officers.

ADJUTANT GENERAL'S OFFICE.
9th May, 1809.

G. O.

1. THE Division under General Sherbrook, General Cotton, General Murray, General Hill, and General
Cameron,

Cameron, will march to-morrow according to routes and instructions already given by the Quarter Master General.

2. The troops will cook this day one day's meat for to-morrow.

3. The Commander of the Forces requests that attention may be paid to the order relative to soldiers marching out of the ranks, and he desires that the files may be counted, and if men are absent the roll shall be called of each Company, when the men will reach their ground after a march, and absentees are to be reported to the Officer commanding Brigades.

4. Captain Charles Doyle, 87th Regiment, is appointed Deputy Assistant Quarter-Master General, until his Majesty's pleasure is known : to bear date from the 9th inst.

ADJUTANT GENERAL's OFFICE.

G. O,   *Convento do Grijon,* 11*th May,* 1809.

2. RETURNS of killed, wounded, and missing, in the skirmishes of the 10th and 11th, to be sent in by the Commanding Officers of regiments, to the Adjutant General's Office, Head Quarters at the Convent of Grijon, this evening, on the left hand side of the road.

3. Officers commanding different columns will give their own orders to the different Commissaries of brigades and regiments respecting the issue of provisions to the troops.

4. The

4. The Commander of the Forces calls the attention of Officers Commanding Regiments and Companies relative to the orders respecting the regularity of march, keeping their Companies collected, not permitting their men to straggle. Lieutenant Colonel Doyle, of the 16th Portuguese, is referred particularly to this order.

The Lieutenant General will send a guard of a Serjeant and eight Portuguese Cavalry to Mr. Boyce, the Pay-Master General, for the safety of the military chest, which he will relieve occasionally; the King's German Legion furnishes the guard of the Commander of the Forces, and a guard of a Corporal and six to the Quarter-Master General and Adjutant General; the French Prisoners taken to be assembled at head quarters immediately, a Serjeant, a Corporal, and twelve men, from the King's German Legion, to take charge of them.

G. O.

ADJUTANT GENERAL's OFFICE.
Oporto, 12th May, 1809.

THE Commander of the Forces congratulates the troops upon the success which has attended their operations for the last four days, upon which they have traversed above eighty miles of most difficult country, in which they have carried some formidable positions, have beat the enemy repeatedly, and have ended by forcing the Passage of the Douro, and defending the position they had so boldly taken up, with numbers far inferior to those with which they were attacked. In the course of this short expedition the Commander of the Forces has had repeated opportunities of witnessing and applauding the gallantry of the Officers

and

and troops, the activity and conduct of the 95th, and of the Light Infantry of the 29th, 43d, and 52d. The bravery of the 16th Portuguese Regiment, the able movement made by Major General Murray with 1st and 2d Battalion Hanoverian Legion, under Brigadier General Langworth, and the gallant attack made by Brigadier General the Hon. Charles Stewart, with a squadron of the 16th, and a squadron of the 20th Light Dragoons, under the command of Major Blake of the 20th, contributed essentially to the success of the attack on the enemy's advanced guard on the 11th, and the steady gallantry of the Buffs, 48th and 16th Regiments, under the command of Major General Hill. The timely passage of the Douro and subsequent movement on the enemy's flank by Lieutenant General Sherbrook, with the brigade of Guards and 29th Regiment, and the bravery of the two squadrons of the 14th Light Dragoons, under the command of Major Harvey, and led by the Hon. Brigadier General Charles Stewart, obtained the victory, which has contributed so much to the honour of the troops on this day. The Commander of the Forces has to express his acknowledgements to the Hon. Lieutenant General Edward Paget, for the manner in which he conducted the advanced guard on the 10th, 11th and 12th, and in which he took up the position beyond the Douro, and he regrets the misfortune which has deprived him (he hopes only for a time) of his assistance.

To Lieutenant General Sherbrook, Major General Murray, Major General Hill; to the Hon. Brigadier General Charles Stewart; to Lieutenant Colonel Delancey, Quarter-Master General's Department, and Captain Mellish, Adjutant General's Department, in the assist-

ance

ance they rendered General Stewart, in his charge of the enemy's defeated Infantry, on the 11th and 12th, and to Major C. Campbell, of the Adjutant General's Department, for the assistance he rendered General Hill, on the defence of his post, and Brigadier General the Hon. Charles Stewart in his charge on the enemy's Infantry, on the 12th.

The Commander of the Forces also acknowledges the assistance he has received from the Adjutant and Quarter-Master General, and the Officers of these departments respectively, and to Lieutenant Colonel Bathurst and the Officers of his personal Staff.

A. G. O.   ADJUTANT GENERAL'S OFFICE.
Oporto, 13th May, 1809.

1. THE following troops are this day or to-morrow morning early, to receive three days bread for the 14th, 15th, and 16th, viz. the brigade of Guards, Brigadier General A. Campbell's, Brigadier General Cameron's, the Cavalry, two brigades of light six-pounders: the horses of the Cavalry, Artillery, Staff, &c. are to receive three days oats or Indian corn for the same time. The above mentioned corps are to march to-morrow morning at such hours, and according to routes which will be sent to them by the Quarter-Master General; they are to cook meat this day for to-morrow.

2. Spare musquet ammunition must be sent with these corps.

3. Major General Hill's and Brigadier General Stew-

art's

arts brigades, the heavy six-pounders, and the reserve Artillery, will halt to-morrow.

4. The detachment of convalescents of different Brigades of the Army, under the command of Major M‘Carthy, of the 97th Regiment, that have arrived this day, will join the same respectively forthwith. Such of the above detachments as have not their Regiments here, will be attached to the 1st Battalion of Detachments till further orders.

G. O.
ADJUTANT GENERAL'S OFFICE.
Oporto, 14th May, 1809.

In the Orders of the 12th instant, it escaped the recollection of the Commander of the Forces to notice the good conduct of the Detachment of the 28th Regiment, under Captain Bradley; on the preceding day, this Detachment conducted itself as became Soldiers of the gallant corps to which they belong.

G. O.
ADJUTANT GENERAL'S OFFICE.
Ruivas, 17th May, 1809.

2. The troops will have observd the extreme difficulty of supplying them with bread in this part of the country, and the necessity that exists, that they should take care of that which is issued to them, and make it last for the time specified in General Orders; for want of attention to this object, and care of their bread, the best operations are necessarily relinquished.

3. On leaving Oporto, the troops had all bread to the
16th,

16th, inclusive; some of them received Bread at Villa Nova, and all one day's bread at Braga, and yet, in this day, they had none : the state of the provisions require the continual superintendance of the Commanding Officers of Regiments, and of the General Officers.

4. Till the army will be in a more plentiful country, the allowance of bread is to be one pound, and one pound and a half of meat each man.

G. O.

ADJUTANT GENERAL'S OFFICE.
San Pedro, 19th May, 1809.

2. THE different brigades will have, at Braga, such men as are unable to march, in charge of an Assistant Surgeon from each brigade, till an Hospital can be established there.

Officers must be left at Braga, in charge of the sick of each brigade, in the proportion of one Subaltern for thirty men, one Captain and one Subaltern for one hundred. A Serjeant must be left in charge of the sick of each Brigade, if the number left should be under thirty, and a Serjeant and Corporal, besides the Officer for each thirty men above the number.

4. When bread cannot be delivered to the troops, they must have two pounds of beef for their ration.

5. It is to be understood by the Soldiers, that wine forms no part of their ration; it is given to them at the pleasure, and upon the responsibility of the Commander of the Forces, and must be discontinued when circumstances prevent its being procured.

6. The ration of bread is to be increased to one pound

and

and a half, by order from the Officers commanding Brigades, as soon as the Assistant Commissaries of Brigades will report that they can make issues to that amount.

7. All horses, mules, bullocks, &c. taken from the enemy, are to be offered for sale to the Commissary General, who will buy them, if they should be found to answer for the Cavalry, the Artillery, or for Commissariat purposes.

8. All purchases of captured horses, mules, &c. contrary to this order, will, in future, be considered null and void, unless they should be purchased by Officers commanding troops or companies, with the knowledge and consent of the General Officers commanding their Brigades, for the purpose of carrying camp kettles, &c.

9. The Officers commanding troops and companies will recollect, that although mules are given to them from the Commissariat, at the commencement of the campaign, they have received an allowance from the public to purchase them, and it was expressly understood that they were to purchase others, if the mules given to them by the Commissariat should be worn out.

10. As the Commander of the Forces has reason to believe many horses and mules are kept by even the Soldiers of the army, and maintained by means entirely inconsistent with discipline and good order, he desires the Officers commanding regiments and brigades to inquire into the number of horses and mules which are attached to the regiments under their command, and to enforce the immediate sale of those not allowed to be kept by the Regulations of the Army.

11. The Commander of the Forces is much concerned to learn, that the unmilitary practice of firing off their pieces in their quarters, which he had attributed entirely to

troops

troops not supposed to be so well disciplined as those of His Majesty, is to be attributed equally to those from whom he expected a better example.

12. The practice of firing off pieces by the Soldiers in their quarters, or at all, but by order of their Officers, is strictly forbid, and any man guilty of it, is to be punished for disobedience of orders.

13. The Soldiers are to be accountable for the quantity of ammunition in their possession, and any man who shall be found to have made away with it, is to be tried and punished.

14. This is not the only irregularity of which the Commander of the Forces has to complain.

15. Under the practice of taking horses from the enemy, the Soldiers have taken them from Portuguese Gentlemen, and have even gone so far as to take two horses belonging to the 16th Light Dragoons, which the Quarter Master General had at Ruivas.

16. The attention of the Officers, commanding Regiments and Brigades, is called particularly to the conduct of the Soldiers under their command.

17. The Officers of companies must attend to their men in their quarters, as well as on a march, or the Army will very soon be no better than a banditti ; if these practices are continued, he desires that Officers, commanding Brigades, will give directions that the Rolls of Companies may be called every hour, and all absentees may be punished. He is, besides, determined that those troops who plunder shall be in the rear instead of in the front of the columns.

18. The Provost is to take charge of all the French prisoners between Montalegre and Braga, a company, 2d

Battalion, 9th Foot, is to be placed at his disposal, and is to meet him to-morrow morning, at day-light, in the village of Villassa, on the high road from Montalegre to Ruivas. The Provost will, this afternoon, move to Villassa all the prisoners at Montalegre; and, on the road between Montalegre and Villassa, he will make requisitions on the Commissary General for such carts as he may require to move the prisoners to Braga, and, in case means should be wanting to move those now on any part of the road, he will leave a small guard in charge of them, and take measures for their subsistence and that of the guard, until he can send conveyances to carry the whole to Braga.

ADJUTANT GENERAL'S OFFICE.

G. O.   *Ruivas, 20th May,* 1809.

1. THE Commander of the Forces calls the attention of the Officers, commanding Brigades and Regiments, to the following Extract of a Letter from the Bishop of Braga; it points out forcibly the necessity which exists, that the Officers of companies should attend to the conduct of the Soldiers under their command, and in what manner want of discipline and good order must defeat the best combined operations.

2. The bread represented to have been irregularly seized by the Soldiers in the rear, was intended for those at the head of the column, who have, therefore, been in want: Commanding Officers of Regiments are held responsible for obedience to the General Orders of the 4th instant, relative to requisitions from the country.

Extract

3. *Extract of a Letter from the Bishop of Braga, to His Excellency Sir Arthur Wellesley.*

I likewise avail myself of this opportunity to inform your Excellency, that notwithstanding my endeavours to procure that supplies of provisions, of all kinds, should be brought forward at this place for the use of the Army under your command, I have not succeeded, until now, to that extent that I promised to do, on account of the arbitrary manner in which the provisions are taken possession of at this place by the different Soldiers of your Excellency's Army, and which prevents a regular return or receipt from being given to the owners. In order, then, to prevent these irregularities, I request that your Excellency will have the goodness to give positive orders, that no person in future, but the Commissaries, are to take possession of the provisions brought in here for the use of the British Army.

I have, &c.

(Signed)   FRANCISCO, Bishop of Braga.

ADJUTANT GENERAL'S OFFICE.
Oporto, 23d May, 1809.

G. O.

1. THE Quarter Master General will forthwith furnish a Corps of Mounted Guides, to be under the immediate superintendance of an Officer of the Quarter-Master General's department; this Corps will receive the pay and allowances of Cavalry, and the Officers, Non-commissioned Officers, and Privates, will be mounted on horses, or

mules,

mules, found by the public. The Corps to be composed as follows:—four Officers receiving the pay and allowances of Lieutenant; four Officers receiving the pay and allowances of Cornet; six Serjeants; six Corporals; two Farriers; and twenty Privates.

2. As the Officers on the Staff of the Adjutant and Quarter Master General's Department are not allowed in Portugal to keep the same number of horses, which are allowed to Officers in the same situations in other parts of the world, and as it is necessary that the communications between the different divisions of the Army should be kept up, in a great degree, through their means, they will be allowed to go post, and to charge for post mules when sent above ten miles from Head-Quarters.

The bill for these charges must, however, be vouched by the signature of the Head of the Department, and farther by a copy of the order to take the journey, specifying the distance.

3. As the General Staff Officers of the Army experienced the greatest difficulty in getting their horses shod, whereby they are frequently disabled from the performance of their duty, the Commander of the Forces will allow of Smiths from the Corps of Infantry being attached, by the permission of the Commanding Officers of the regiments to which they belong, to the Officers hereinafter named, to shoe the horses of the General Staff Officers under their command, or in the neighbourhood of their stations, viz. Lieutenant General Sherbrooke; Major General Murray; Major General Hill. These Officers will each be allowed to draw forage for one mule to carry the implements and tools of the Smith: the mule must be provided by those who will benefit by the establishment.

blishment. Two Smiths are also to be attached in the same manner to the Commandant at Head Quarters, to shoe the horses of all the Staff.

7. A small sum of money being arrived, the Paymaster General will issue a proportion to regiments on the application of their respective Paymasters.

8. The following Staff Officers not having appeared in Orders to be obeyed accordingly :—Captain G. Dalbiac, 4th Dragoons ; Lieutenant Edward Burk, 18th Light Dragoons; Aides de-Camp to Lieutenant General Payne ; and Ensign Honourable Fitzgibbon, extra Aide-de-Camp to ditto ;—Captain James Stewart, 95th Regiment ; Captain George Marlay, 2d Garrison Battalion, Aides-de-Camp to Lieutenant General the Honourable E. Paget ; Captain Marquis of Tweedale, 1st Guards, extra Aide-de-Camp to ditto ; Lieutenant George Fitzclarence, 10th Light Dragoons, Aide-de-Camp to Brigadier General the Honourable Charles Stewart.

9. On the arrival of the Army at Aveiro, where the ship with medical stores has been detained, every Surgeon, whether Staff or Regimental, is immediately to renew and complete all deficiencies in any part of the original field equipment, directed in General Orders.

The Commissary General will replace, on application, any of those public mules that have been so injured as to be unserviceable.

General Officers, commanding Brigades, are requested to facilitate, as much as possible, the conveyance of what has been ordered during the approaching march, as the succour of the sick, and the preservation of the wounded in the field, must, in a great degree, depend upon what regiments carry with them.

10. Pur-

10. Purveyor's Clerk Henry Bacon, is appointed Acting Deputy Purveyor to the Forces.

ADJUTANT GENERAL'S OFFICE.
Oporto, 23d May, 1809.

A. G. O.

1. THE Commander of the Forces has been informed, and, indeed, has observed, notwithstanding the orders issued by the late Commander of the Forces and himself, much of the private baggage of the Army is moved upon bullock cars. The Officers must have felt the inconvenience which this mode of transporting their baggage must be to themselves personally. It is scarcely possible that the baggage can keep up with them, even at present, and when the Army will move in larger divisions, will become quite impossible.

The public inconvenience resulting from this mode of transporting private baggage is still greater. The Commander of the Forces is aware that in forced marches, and in bad weather it may happen that animals provided for carriage will knock up, but hopes that Officers of the Army will consider it as a determined measure, that no baggage is to be carried upon bullock cars, excepting those allowed by the late Commander of the Forces, and that those who have baggage to carry, must be provided with mules or horses.

2. In addition to the ration ordered for the Portuguese troops by the General Orders at Coimbra, they are to receive, each man, one pint of wine per diem, in the same manner as those in the service of His Majesty.

G. O.

G. O.

1. THE different Brigades will send to Oporto, forthwith, the proportion of Officers, Non-commissioned Officers, and Hospital Servants, required to take charge of the sick in Hospital, according to the proportion ordered by the General Orders of the 19th instant.

2. The Army being likely to go into huts at an early period, the Commander of the Forces is disposed to supply the Officers with tents from the public stores, in the proportion of one tent for each Field Officer, and one tent for the Officers of each company, and one for the Staff; it will be necessary, however, that the Officers, to whom these tents will be issued, shall provide means for the carriage, without encreasing the demands for forage.

3. The Officers commanding Regiments will send to the Quarter Master General, through the Officers commanding their Brigades, returns of the names of those Officers who are desirous of having tents, stating the numbers required for the regiments under their command, according to the proportions above specified.

4. Mr. Domenique de Francisco is attached to the Quarter Master General's Department, with the pay and allowances of Lieutenant of Cavalry; appointment dated 10th May. Captain George Humphreys, 3d Battalion, 27th Regiment, is appointed Deputy Assistant Quarter Master General, from the 24th instant.

G. O.

ADJUTANT GENERAL'S OFFICE.
25th *May,* 1809.

G. O.

1. THE German Hussars and the 23d Dragoons, when they shall arrive, are to form a brigade under the command of Major General Erskine.

2. Captain Serle, of the 24th regiment, is appointed Brigade Major to the brigade of cavalry under the command of Major General Erskine.

3. The battalion of Portuguese regiment, hitherto attached to General Cameron's brigade, are to form part of the garrison of Oporto, and are to remain here under the command of Lieutenant Colonel Trant.

ADJUTANT GENERAL'S OFFICE.
Ovea, 26th *May,* 1809.

G. O.

1. THE Commander of the Forces begs that the Officers commanding brigades will ascertain the number of men left behind, on the march, by each of the regiments under their command, from the time the army left Coimbra ; and they will make a return of them to the Adjutant General's Office, stating the names of the Officers commanding the companies from which those men have absented themselves.

ADJUTANT

ADJUTANT GENERAL's OFFICE,
Coimbra, 29th May, 1809.

G. O.

THE Commander of the Forces is much concerned to be obliged again to complain of the conduct of the troops; not only have outrages been committed by whole corps, but there is no description of property of which the unfortunate inhabitants of Portugal have not been plundered by the British soldiers, whom they have received into their houses, or by stragglers from the different regiments of the army. The Commander of the Forces apprehends, that the interior discipline of the regiments is materially relaxed, and he therefore desires that the soldiers of every company, in each of the regiments, may be formed into as many squads as there are Non-commissioned Officers, each squad having in it one Non-commissioned Officer, who must be responsible for the conduct of the soldiers in his squad.

The Non-Commissioned Officers must always be quartered with the men of their squads.

On halting days an Officer of each company must visit the quarters of the men of his company, four times each day, of which one must be at eight o'clock in the evening. On marching days an officer of each company must visit the quarters, twice after the men have got into them, of which once must be at eight o'clock in the evening. An Officer must also visit the quarters of the company, before the soldiers march in the morning.

The object of these visitings is to see that the soldiers conduct themselves regularly in their quarters, to ascertain whether there are any complaints by the landlords, and of

whom,

whom, and that the men are in their quarters, instead of marauding in search of plunder.

The Officers of the companies, who will visit, must report to the Commanding Officer that they have visited the quarters the number of times ordered, specifying the number.

The Commanding Officer will report daily to the Officer commanding the brigade, that these visitings have been made. The Officers must be quartered in the immediate neighbourhood of their companies.

The Commander of the Forces calls the attention of the Officers commanding brigades and regiments to the orders given out, and repeated, with a view to prevent the soldiers from straggling from their regiments on a march, which have hitherto been ineffectual. He desires that a report of absentees may be made after every march to the Officer commanding the brigade; and the Officer commanding the brigade will send this report, with a statement from what companies the men are absent, to the Commander of the Forces.

The use of carts to carry baggage of any description, is again positively forbid; and it is equally forbid to have guards with any baggage.

The hospital bedding and stores heretofore carried under charge of Regimental Surgeons, is to be sent into the hospital at Coimbra; there will be only one cart attached to each regiment, viz. that to carry men who may fall sick on a march; no guard whatever must be out of the ranks on a march, excepting those ordered by the General Orders.

No soldier must be employed to press carts or bullocks,

for

for draught or food, excepting accompanied and directed by the Assistant Commissary of the brigade, or his Deputy or Clerk, except in cases of evident necessity; when the Commanding Officer of the brigade, in the absence of the Assistant Commissary, may direct that carts or bullocks for draught or food may be pressed, in which case an Officer must command the party; and the Officer commanding the brigade must report the circumstance, as soon as possible, to head-quarters.

The circumstances which have occasioned these orders have given the Commander of the Forces the greatest concern; and he hopes, with the assistance of the Officers of the army, to put an end to the disgraceful practices which have prevailed.

The people of Portugal deserve well of the army; they have in every instance treated the soldiers well; and there never was an army so well supplied, or which had so little excuse for plunder, if any excuse can in any case exist. But if the Commander of the Forces should not by these and other measures be enabled to get the better of these practices, he is determined to report to his Majesty, and send into garrison those corps who shall continue them; as he prefers a small but disciplined and well ordered body of troops to a rabble however numerous; and he is resolved not to be the instrument of inflicting upon the people of this country the miseries which result from the operations of such a body.

The regulations of these Orders are to be understood as applicable to the dragoons and the artillery, as well as the infantry.

ADJUTANT

ADJUTANT GENERAL'S OFFICE.

G. O.   *Coimbra, 30th May, 1809.*

THE following appointments have taken place, to bear date from the 25th instant.

James Dickens, Esq. to be Deputy Commissary of Accounts.

Joseph Holyworth Adams, Esq. Assistant Commissary of Accounts.

George Ainslie, Esq. Acting Assistant Commissary of Accounts.

The Commander of the Forces omitted to mention in the Orders of the 12th instant, after the action, the good conduct of the rifle corps under Major Wurmb, that was with the 1st brigade King's German Legion; his Excellency had every reason to be satisfied with those excellent troops.

1. All hospital stoppages now due in Coimbra to be paid as soon as possible; and hereafter, when regiments leave sick in hospital, they are always to settle with the hospital, up to the 24th of the month.

2. The Commanding Officers of those regiments which are in want of any articles now in the regimental stores at Lisbon, will send to the Quarter-Master General a list of the articles so required, stating where they are to be found, and the name of the person in charge of them; Heads of Departments will do the same.

3. The rations of all the mules and horses with the army, is hereafter to be as follows:

14 lbs. of hay or straw.

12 lbs. of oats, or 10 lbs. of Indian corn or barley.

4. Captain George Elliot, 48th regiment, is removed from the Adjutant General's, to the Quarter-Master General's Department.

ADJUTANT

ADJUTANT GENERAL'S OFFICE.
Coimbra, 31st May, 1809.

G. O.

1. THERE being now 6000 pairs of shoes, the Officers commanding brigades will direct the Officers commanding regiments in their brigades, to make a requisition to the Assistant Commissary attached to the brigade, for the number of pairs of shoes they will require to complete the men; but no regiment is to require more than one pair of shoes for each man. These shoes are to be paid for at the rate of 6*s*. 6*d*. per pair.

2. The regiments are to make a requisition on the Quarter-Master General for bill-hooks, in the proportion of one for every ten men; these bill-hooks are to be carried by the soldiers, under the straps of the knapsack, outside. The troops will very soon experience the use of them, and must take the greatest care of them; they must be produced by the men at every inspection of necessaries. A return of them must be made to the Quarter Master General, once a month; and any deficiencies of the numbers not accounted for in a satisfactory manner, must be made good by the companies to which the bill-hooks have been delivered.

3. Those regiments in want of camp kettles, will make a requisition for them upon the Quarter-Master General; deficiencies must however be accounted for in a satisfactory manner: in future a return of camp kettles must be sent to the Quarter-Master General on the first of every month; likewise returns monthly of haversacks and canteens to him. The regiments will make a requisition for the numbers they now want to complete; a satisfactory account must be given of the deficiencies.

4. A

4. A General Court Martial will assemble to-morrow morning, at seven o'clock, for the trial of such prisoners as may be brought before it.

Major General Hill, President.

	Field Officers.	Captains.	Subalterns.
Major Gen. Hill's Brigade . .	1 —	2 —	0
Brig. Gen. A. Campbell's do. .	2 —	1 —	0
Brig. Gen. R. Stewart's do. . .	1 —	2 —	2
Brig. Gen. Sontag's do. . . .	0 —	1 —	2
Total . .	4 —	6 —	4

Major General Hill's brigade will appoint an Officer to act as Deputy Judge Advocate; the prisoners to be warned, and all evidences to attend. A list of evidences, and names, and dates of commissions of the Officers composing the Court Martial, to be sent to the Deputy Judge Advocate, at General Hill's quarters, this evening.

ADJUTANT GENERAL'S OFFICE.
Coimbra, 1st June, 1809.

G. O.

1. THE Commander of the Forces has been informed that the Officers commanding companies, and other regimental Officers, having been supplied with mules by the Commissariat, by order of the late Commander of the Forces, for the carriage of camp kettles, of Paymasters' books, and of the medicine chest, when the army took the field, have applied to have those mules exchanged.

The

The Officers commanding companies, Paymasters, and Surgeons, must be aware that they receive an allowance from the public to furnish mules or horses for the carriage of camp kettles, books, or medicine chests; they are reminded by the Orders of the 11th October, the 18th of March, and 19th of May, that these mules were given to them by the Commissariat only as an indulgence, and that they were to keep them up at their own charge; and under these circumstances it is impossible for the Commissary General now to exchange them.

2. The mule attached to each regiment for the carriage of the entrenching tools, and placed by the Orders of the 16th March in charge of the Quarter-Master, belongs to the public, and he must be exchanged by the Commissary, if the exchange should be necessary, (which it ought not to be.) It is clearly understood, that although the camp kettle mules, and those for the books and medicine chests, are to be kept up the Captains, Paymaster, and Surgeons, respectively, they must not be used for any purpose, excepting those for which they are exclusively allowed.

4. Regiments are to receive each of them, as soon as possible, a sum of money from the Paymaster General at Coimbra.

6. Although from circumstances it is at present impossible to supply the Paymasters of regiments with money to the full amount of their estimates, and the Captains of companies have not yet received the full amount of pay of their several companies for the last month, no reason exists why the accounts of the soldiers should not be settled to the 24th of the month of May, and the balances

struck

struck, which will be paid off as soon as the money shall come up.

7. The Paymaster General will advance to the Surgeon of the general hospital at Coimbra, the sum of 300*l.* on account, which will be repaid by the Surgeon, when he will receive the hospital stoppages from the different regiments.

8. An Officer from the 7th, 53d, 29th, and 1st battalion detachments to proceed forthwith by the road of Aveiro, Oporto, and Braga, to look for the men who have been allowed to straggle from those regiments, according to the return sent in to the Adjutant General's Office, copies of which they are to be furnished with by the Officers commanding the corps.

The Commander of the Forces trusts that more attention will be paid by the Officers commanding companies to prevent the soldiers from straggling in future.

11. Officers commanding regiments will transmit to the Adjutant General's Office the usual weekly states, notwithstanding the General Orders of the 6th February, on the 1st, 8th, and 15th days of each month respectively.

ADJUTANT GENERAL'S OFFICE.

PASS ORDER. *Coimbra, 1st June,* 1809.

The battalions of Portuguese troops attached to the British brigades on the late march, are to be left at Coimbra, and not proceed with them.

The General Court Martial, of which Major General Hill was President, is dissolved, the proceedings having been approved of by the Commander in Chief.

Memo-

Memorandum.—The receipt of this order to be acknowledged by the brigade Majors, who copy it for their respective brigades.

G. O.　　　　ADJUTANT GENERAL'S OFFICE.
　　　　　　　Coimbra, 2d June, 1809.

CAPTAIN Humphreys, of the 27th Regiment, to be Deputy Assistant Quarter-Master General, from the 25th May; Captain Harvey, 53d Foot, to be Deputy Assistant Quarter-Master General from the 1st June, and attached to Marshal Beresford.

1. A General Court Martial, held at Coimbra, on the 1st June, 1809, of which Major General Rowland Hill was President, proceeded to the trial of Doderick Gerlock, a private Soldier in the 5th Battalion 60th Regiment of Foot, for deserting from the 5th Battalion 60th Regiment of Foot, on or about the 1st of February last, on the road from Lanego to Oporto, and entering the French Service, from which he was taken prisoner in Portugal, on or about the 17th May.

The prisoner being arraigned and pleading not guilty, the Court proceeded to the examination of witnesses, and having maturely weighed the evidences against the prisoner, together with what he had to allege in his defence, were of opinion that he was Guilty of the crime laid to his charge, in breach of the Articles of War; and did therefore adjudge him, Dodrick Gerlock, to be hanged or shot to death, at such time and place as it shall please the Commander of the Forces to direct; which sentence has been confirmed by His Excellency Lieutenant General Sir Arthur Wellesley, Commander of the Forces.

The same Court next proceeded to the trial of private Henry Drum, 32d regiment, confined by order of Lieutenant General Sherbrooke, for robbing at Aveiro, on the 27th of May last: the prisoner being arraigned, pleaded not guilty. The Court proceeded to the examination of witnesses, and having maturely weighed the evidence against the prisoner, together with what he had to urge in his defence, were of opinion that he is not guilty of the crime laid to his charge, and do therefore acquit him of the same; which sentence has been confirmed by His Excellency Lieutenant General Sir Arthur Wellesley Commander of the Forces.

2. The sentence of the General Court Martial on Doderick Gerlock, of the 5th battalion 60th regiment, is to be carred into execution this evening at five o'clock, in the open space beyond the bridge, on the road leading to Oporto. All the companies of the 5th battalion 60th regiment, a company of each regiment now at Coimbra, the whole under the command of a Field Officer, will parade on the spot at half past four to see the sentence executed.

The Field Officer and the Provost Marshal will receive orders from the Adjutant General respecting the execution; a guard of a serjeant and twelve to be left on the ground after the execution is over.

3. The Order No. 2, of the 30th May, has not been attended to, no regiment having yet sent to the Quarter Master General any account of articles required from Lisbon. The earliest attention must be given to all Orders. In this instance, the regiments may feel the greatest incon-

venience

venience for want of those articles in store at Lisbon, with which it was the intention of the orders of 30th May to supply, which articles they cannot get by any other means.

4. Whenever Sick are left in Hospital at any place, the strictest attention must be paid, that Officers and Non-commissioned Officers of each brigade are left in charge of them, according to the proportion ordered in General Orders of the 19th May, for the hospital at Braga.

5. The following Gentlemen are appointed to the corps of Guides, from the 25th May—Thomas de Auguino Guiseppe de Carnalho, with the pay of Lieutenant; Carlos Perigrono Belfant de Burgos, with the pay of Lieutenant; Antonio Rasemondo Belfond de Burgos, with the pay of Cornet; Agastino Albano da Silvero with the pay of Cornet.

———————

ADJUTANT GENERAL'S OFFICE.
G. O.   *Coimbra, 3d June, 1809.*

1. MR. John Malone is appointed to the corps of Guides, with the pay and allowances of Cornet from the 3d instant.

2. Whenever it is possible for the Assistant Commissaries of brigades to issue the quantity, cavalry must receive and carry three days corn, and the infantry three days bread.

3. The senior of the Officers left in charge of the sick at the different hospitals must take the command of the whole, and correspond with head quarters; no convalescents must be moved from any hospital station without orders from head quarters.

E 2

4. The

4. The following detachments having arrived from the Isle of Wight, at Lisbon, Officers commanding regiments will report to the Adjutant General's Office, whether they have the means of equipping the same with arms and accoutrements, and will send any directions for that purpose to the Quarter-Master General's Office, which will be forwarded to Lisbon previous to the detachment being ordered to Abrantes, where they will join their respective corps.

Detail of Detachments.

	Captains.	Lieutenants.	Ensigns.	Serjeants.	Corporals.	Privates.	
3d Regt. or Buffs		0	0	0	0	2	No arms or accoutr.
24th do. 2d Batt.	4	2	2	3	6	209	Have arms but no acc.
7th do. do.	0	0	0	0	0	1	
27th do. 3d Batt.	0	0	0	0	0	4	
29th do.	0	0	1	5	3	60	
31st do. 2d Batt.	0	0	0	0	1	10	
40th do. 1st Batt.	0	0	0	0	3	67	
45th do. 1st Batt.	0	0	0	0	0	5	No arms or accoutr.
53d do. 2d Batt.	0	0	0	0	0	1	
60th do. 5th Batt.	0	0	0	0	0	1	
83d do. 2d Batt.	0	0	0	0	0	2	
88th do. 1st Batt.	0	0	0	0	0	1	
97th do.	0	0	0	0	0	3	
King's German Legion	0	1	1	2	1	31	One private of these a deserter with arms and accoutrements complete, the remainder without.

ADJUTANT

ADJUTANT GENERAL'S OFFICE.
Coimbra, 4th June, 1809.

G. O.

1. THE men of the regiments of the brigade of Guards and General Cameron's brigade may receive from the Commissariat Stores, each two pair of shoes, if their Commanding Officer choose to make requisitions for them, to be paid for at the rate of 6s. 6d. per pair.

ADJUTANT GENERAL'S OFFICE.
Thomar, 7th June, 1809.

G. O.

ORDERS having been received from the War Office directing that the hospital stoppages, from all ranks, should be nine pence instead of ten pence per diem ; this order is to take effect from the 25th June inclusive.

Brevet Major E. B. I. Green, of the 10th regiment, is appointed an Assistant Quarter-Master General, and Captain S. T. Wittingham, of the 13th Light Dragoons, Deputy Assistant Quarter-Master General, from the 25th April last.

HORSE GUARDS.
12th May, 1809.

SIR,

HAVING laid before the King the proceedings of a General Court Martial held at Camarata on the 21st and 22d March, 1809, for the trial of Lieutenant Edward Keating of the 45th regiment, who was arraigned upon the following charges, viz.

With

With conduct unbecoming the character of an Officer and a Gentleman, on the night of 15th March, 1809, when Subaltern of the Piquet, in using most abusive language towards his superior officer, Captain Lightfoot of the same corps, at that time commanding the said piquet, being a direct breach of the Articles of War, and totally subversive of good order and military discipline.

Upon which charge, the Court came to the following decision.

The Court having maturely weighed and considered the evidence against the prisoner Lieutenant Edward Keating, 45th regiment, as well as what he hath urged in his defence, are of opinion that he is guilty of the crime laid to his charge, being a breach of the articles of war; and do therefore sentence him, the said Lieutenant Edward Keating, 45th regiment, to be cashiered.

I am to acquaint you that His Majesty approved and confirmed the sentence of the Court: you will therefore acquaint me with the day upon which the sentence is made known to the prisoner Lieutenant Keating, as from that day he will cease to receive pay in His Majesty's service.

I have the honour to be,

Sir,

Your most obedient humble servant,

(Signed)   D. DUNDAS,

Commander in Chief.

ADJUTANT GENERAL'S OFFICE.

Abrantes, 8th June, 1809.

G. O.

THE regiments will make a requisition upon the Commissary

missary at Abrantes for a sufficient number of pairs of Shoes to complete them to two good pairs each man, the period of the delivery of those shoes will be notified in General Orders ; they will be paid at the rate of 6s. 6d. per pair. The regiments not already completed with bill hooks, canteens, haversacks, and camp kettles, according to the General Orders of the 31st ultimo, will make a requisition upon the Quarter-Master General, at Abrantes, for the same ; the period of the delivery of those articles will likewise be notified in General Orders.

2. Various complaints having been made to the Commander of the Forces, of the irregularity of the delivery of articles from the Commissariat, the following rules are to be observed upon that subject in future.

3. When articles are delivered to troops from a General Store, the Commissary General must, if possible, have two or more stores for the delivery of each article, viz. forage, corn, wood, meat, bread, and wine.

4. He must signify to the Assistant Commissaries of brigades and regiments, at which store, and where situated, Troops in the brigade or regiment will receive their supplies, and in what order by brigades, and at what hour the supplies will be delivered to the troops of each brigade or regiment at each store.

5. In general however, it is better the troops of each brigade or regiment should receive their supplies at the brigade or regimental store.

6. When the army will halt, a commencement must be made to make the deliveries at the Commissaries stores at day-light, and the delivery must be continued without interruption, till the whole of the troops to receive their supplies at such store shall have received them. The sol-

diers

diers of each brigade or regiment will attend to receive the supplies at the hour appointed for them precisely, and not before.

7. The meat for the troops must invariably be delivered to them from a brigade or regimental store, and should be killed on the preceding night, or at day-light in the morning, when the army halts.

When it marches, the order of the 5th of May comes in force, and the meat should be killed, delivered, and cooked, as soon as possible after the orders for marching are given out.

8. When the army marches, the Commissary General should notify as soon as possible to the Assistant Commissaries of brigades and regiments of cavalry, where the store of each article of supply for the troops will be made to each brigade or regiment. The deliveries on marching days must commence as soon as possible after the troops reach their ground.

9. It is obvious however, that on marching days it is still more important than it is on halting days, that the delivery should be made from a brigade or regimental, rather than a general store.

10. The Assistant Commissaries with regiments of cavalry and brigades must not be changed, unless the change is notified in General Orders.

11. The Assistant Commissaries with brigades and regiments of cavalry must take care to obtain copies of all General Orders from the Brigade Majors, or Adjutants respectively. The Commissary General is responsible that all other Officers of the Department, not attached to brigades or regiments of cavalry, have copies of the General Orders.

ADJUTANT

ADJUTANT GENERAL'S OFFICE.
Abrantes, 10th June, 1809.

G. O.

1. THE baggage of the army is immediately to be disembarked from the transports in the Tagus, and to be placed in stores at Lisbon; each regiment will, as soon as possible, send to Lisbon an Officer or a careful non-commissioned officer, to superintend the removal of the baggage belonging to the regiment, to the store-house allotted to receive it; these Officers and non-commissioned Officers will report themselves on their arrival at Lisbon to the Assistant Quarter-Master General stationed there, and will receive his directions respecting the store-house to be allotted for the baggage of the Regiment, the means of removing it from the transports to the store-house, and those for arranging it there.

2. After the baggage shall have been placed in the store-houses at Lisbon, it must be in charge of one non-commissioned Officer or steady Private Soldier of each regiment, who is to be left there, and all the other Officers and non-commissioned Officers sent to Lisbon respecting baggage, must return to join the army.

3. Mr. Acting Assistant Commissary Strachan is removed from the charge of Brigadier General Campbell's brigade for other services; Mr. Wemyss, Commissariat Department, is appointed to Brigadier General Campbell's brigade in his room.

Memorandum.—Should any regiment have Officers or non-commissioned Officers at Lisbon, who can perform the duty relative to regimental baggage, Officers commanding regiments will send instructions to them,

agree-

agreeable to the General Orders from hence, and there will be no occasion for regiments to detach persons for the above duty.

5. The Commander of the Forces having been pleased to order ten pounds bât money to be allowed to Regimental Surgeons, on the issue of 200 days bât and forage money, such regiments as have not already drawn the same, will immediatly send in supplementary returns for it to the Quarter-Master General.

As the cisterns in the town of Abrantes are all sealed and closed up, with a view to the preservation of the water which they contain, for the purpose of the fortification which is to be erected here, the Soldiers must not touch them; several of the cisterns having been already broken open by the Soldiers, notwithstanding that they were sealed and locked up. The Officers commanding Regiments are requested to visit the quarters occupied by their corps, to see that all the cisterns are again locked up and sealed, and a sentry must be placed over each.

The troops must bring from the river the water which they require.

ADJUTANT GENERAL'S OFFICE.

G. O.   *Abrantes, 11th June,* 1809.

1. MAJOR General Hill's and Brigadier General Stewart's brigades will move out of Abrantes to-morrow, into huts, which they will construct, on ground which will be pointed out to them by an Officer of the Quarter-Master General's Department.

2. When the army is in cantonments, the following

rules

rules are to be observed in respect to quarters : the allot-
ments of the quarters of any considerable corps of the
army is to be made by the Officer commanding it, through
the Assistant Quarter-Master General attached to the
corps, or in his absence through any other Officer of his
Staff; no individual is to take quarters for himself, or
change them, without the authority of the Officer commanding in the cantonments. The Staff and other un-
attached Officers are to be quartered by the Assistant Quarter Master General of the corps of the army
to which they belong, or the Officer acting for him. Regimental Officers are to take their quarters in the street or
district allotted to their respective corps ; but when a Regiment is placed in any public building, which does not
afford accommodation for Officers, such as are not ordered
to remain with the men will have quarters allotted to them.
All regulations respecting quarters in the town or village
where the head quarters of the army are established, are
to be made by the Commandant at head quarters.

3. All men able to march, whether convalescents from
the hospital at Lisbon, or men lately arrived there from
England, who have arms and accoutrements, will be ordered to join their Regiments, and 150 men of the 2d
battalion of the 24th regiment; and 50 men of each of
the regiments of the army of those lately arrived, who have
no arms or accoutrements, will likewise join the army;
no man of the 2d Battalion of the 9th, or 3d Battalion
of the 27th will move from Lisbon.

The Quarter-Master General at Lisbon will give routes,
and those men of each regiment will join, as they pass
through the cantonments of their regiments. Brigadier
General A. Campbell's brigade will furnish the public
duties to-morrow.

Adju-

G. O. ADJUTANT GENERAL's OFFICE.
Abrantes, 12*th June,* 1809.

1. WHEN bedding is required for the sick, whether Regimental or general Hospitals, and it cannot be supplied by the general stores, the Surgeon in charge of the hospital must make a requisition in writing for what he requires to the Commissary of the Brigade, or the Commissary General: the Officer of the Commissariat will make a requisition upon the Magistrate of the place, for what will thus be required by the Surgeon; the Surgeon will give his receipt for the bedding delivered to him, and he will be responsible to return the whole of the bedding to the Magistrate who procured it.

2. His Majesty has been pleased to appoint Dr. Haine to be on the Medical Staff with this army; Surgeon Leonis Le Court and Mr. Leonis Augustus Le Court are also appointed to the Medical Staff of the army, to be employed for the medical attendance of French Prisoners. Staff Surgeon Haine to bear date from the 25th June; Messrs. Le Court from the 25th July. Staff Surgeon Quintley has also been appointed to the Hospital Staff of the army; to bear date from the 25th June.

3. The undermentioned Departments will henceforward make up their own pay abstracts, and transmit them to the Military Secretary, instead of their being included in the abstract of the Staff, made up hitherto by the Quarter-Master General, viz.

 Commissary Department.
 Medical Ditto.
 Commissary of Accounts.

4. A

4. A General Court Martial will assemble on the 15th instant, at Barquinha, for the trial of such prisoners as may be brought before it.

Brigadier General Langworth, President.

	Field Officers.	Captains.	Subalterns.
Brigade of Guards - - - - - - - -	2 —	1 —	0
Br. Gen. Cameron's Brigade - -	0 —	2 —	2
Maj. Gen. Murray's Division - -	2 —	3 —	2
Total - - - -	4 —	6 —	4

Capt. Giles, 3d Guards, Deputy Judge Advocate.

The prisoners to be warned, and all evidences to attend; a list of evidences and names and dates of the Officers commissions composing the Court Martial, to be sent to the Deputy Judge Advocate, at Brigadier General Langworth's quarters, on the 14th instant.

5. The detachment of the 40th Regiment arrived this day at Abrantes, will be attached to the 97th Regiment, until the arrival of their own corps.

G. O.
ADJUTANT GENERAL'S OFFICE.
Abrantes, 13th June, 1809.

THE senior Officer in charge of the sick at Oporto and Coimbra, will once a week send by the Post to head quarters, a return of the sick, specifying the number of recovered men able to march.

The Commanding Officers of those Regiments of the army, to the men of which clothing is due, will report to
the

the Quarter-Master General whether the clothing is arrived at Lisbon and where.

1. Whenever 40 men at either hospital are sufficiently recovered to be able to march, an order and a route will be sent for their march by easy stages.

2. They are to take with them at setting out, three days bread in biscuit, which they are to keep by them as a reserve.

3. The Commissary General will arrange that they shall be fed at the different halting places.

4. An Officer must be sent in command of every detachment of 40 men, and two Officers if the number should amount to 80, and so on; one Officer for every 40 in addition; one non-commissioned Officer must be sent for every 20 sick; and the Commanding Officer at the hospital must make arrangements that other Officers and non-commissioned Officers should take charge of the remaining sick of the brigade, in charge of which such Officer or non-commissioned Officer have been left at the hospital.

5. The senior Officer at the hospital will report to the Quarter-Master General the departure of the recovered men; and Officers commanding the party of recovered men must report their progress to head quarters by every opportunity.

6. Brigadier-General Campbell's and Sontag's brigades are to move into huts to-morrow morning, on ground that will be pointed out to them by the Quarter-Master General.

7. The Commander of the Forces requests that olive and other fruit trees may not be used by the troops in hutting, except in case of evident necessity.

8. If

8. If the country in the neighbourhood of the several cantonments, should afford materials fit for hutting, the Commander of the Forces is desirous that the troops should be moved into huts as soon as possible; the Officers commanding Brigades will make arrangements accordingly. The tents will be delivered to the Officers who have made requisitions for them, under the orders of the 24th May, as soon as they shall arrive from Lisbon.

9. All Commissaries and other persons who have Portuguese Dragoons attached to them, are to send the Dragoons to Abrantes immediately, reporting to the Adjutant General that they have done so.

10. The Commander of the Forces is concerned to have to announce to the army that Private Richard Jew, of the 53d regiment, has been wounded, and has probably died of the wounds he received from some peasants in the neighbourhood of Coimbra; and that Corporal Booth and Private Gilbert Wyatt have probably met with the same fate: this is one of the consequences of the irregularities of which the soldiers have been guilty, which have had the effect of turning into enemies a people who were grateful for the benefits which they had received from the British nation, and manifested their gratitude by affording to the soldiers every comfort and assistance which was in their power.

The Commanding Officers of brigades and regiments are particularly requested to point out to the soldiers the consequences of their irregularities.

12. Mr. John Winter to act as Deputy Purveyor to the forces until further orders.

Mr. Amril is appointed to act as Extra Hospital Mate

to

to the forces from the 10th instant, and to report himself to Colonel Trant at Oporto, to attend the sick and wounded prisoners to England.

'Captain J. Mine is appointed Brigade Major to Brigadier General Howorth, vice Dickum, from the date hereof.

G. O.
ADJUTANT GENERAL'S OFFICE.
Abrantes, 14th June, 1809.

1. SERJEANT FOLLOWS, 3d Guards, is appointed Provost Marshal to the army, vice Enzinger resigned, from the date hereof.

A. G. O.
ADJUTANT GENERAL'S OFFICE.
Abrantes, 14th June, 1809.

COLONEL DONKIN is appointed to the Command of the Brigade of Infantry lately under the Orders of Major General Tilson.

His Excellency has been pleased to appoint Colonel Peacock, of the 1st Battalion Coldstream Guards, to be a Colonel on the Staff of the Army until his Majesty's pleasure is known; and he is appointed to the Command of the Brigade of Infantry lately under the orders of Brigadier General Sontag.

ADJUTANT

G. O.   *Abrantes, 15th June, 1809.*

A GENERAL Court Martial to assemble to-morrow morning at 11 o'clock, for the trial of such prisoners as may be brought before it.

Brigadier General A. Campbell, President.

	Field Officers.	Captains.	Subalterns.
Brig. Gen. Fane's Brigade . . .	2 —	0 —	1
Major Gen. Hill's ditto	1 —	2 —	2
Brig. Gen. A. Campbell's ditto .	0 —	2 —	0
Brig. Gen. R. Stewart's ditto . .	0 —	1 —	1
Colonel Peacock's ditto	1 —	1 —	0
Total . . .	4 —	6 —	4

Brigadier General Campbell's brigade will be pleased to furnish an Officer to act as Deputy Judge Advocate, who will be appointed (if approved) by the Commander of the Forces.

List of the evidences, names and dates of commissions of the Officers composing the court martial, to be sent to Brigadier General Campbell's quarters, this evening; the prisoners to be warned, and all evidences to attend.

2. The 2d battalion 9th regiment is to proceed to Lisbon by such routes as will be delivered to them by the Quarter-Master General.

3. The 40th regiment is to proceed from Lisbon by water to Santarem, and from thence to Tancos by land, by such routes as may be delivered to them by the Quarter-Master General; the 40th regiment will form part of

the brigade under the orders of Brigadier General Cameron.

4. The 2d battalion 24th regiment will be in General M‘Kenzie's brigade.

5. The following gentlemen are attached to the corps of Guides from the 26th May, with the pay and allowances of Cornets:

> Rodrigo de Francisco Magollens.
> John Antonio de Sylon.

6. A board of Field Officers of King's German Legion will sit at Barquintia without loss of time, under the directions of Brigadier General Langworth, to report upon the shoes of the brigade reported unfit for service.

7. A division of Apothecary's stores having arrived at head-quarters, Surgeons of regiments are immediately to complete their field panniers with whatever has been directed, by requisitions to the Inspector of Hospitals at head-quarters.

8. All the men of the 40th regiment at Abrantes, are to be attached to the 97th foot till the arrival of their own corps.

G. O.

ADJUTANT GENERAL'S OFFICE.
Abrantes, 16th June, 1809.

1. Two more Assistant Provosts will be appointed; Commanding Officers of brigades will please to send in recommendations of men capable of filling the situation: one of the Assistant Provosts is to repair to the camp near Abrantes, and to report himself to the Officer commanding the camp. He will patrole round the neighbourhood

bourhood of it, and will take up all stragglers and marauders; two dragoons are to be attached to this Provost, and to be relieved daily.

2. An Assistant Provost is to proceed to Castello Branco, and to place himself under the orders of Colonel Donkin.

3. Lieutenant Colonel Elley, A. A. General, is appointed to the cavalry under the command of Lieutenant General Payne; he will report himself to him accordingly. Captain Cotton, Deputy Assistant Adjutant General, will return to the duties of the department at head-quarters.

ADJUTANT GENERAL'S OFFICE.
Abrantes, 17th June, 1809.

G. O.

ERRATUM in the Orders of the 15th June.

Read—Brigadier General Campbell's brigade will be pleased to furnish an Officer to act as Deputy Judge Advocate, who will be appointed, if approved of by the Commander of the Forces, instead of, Brigadier General Campbell will be pleased to appoint an Officer to act as Deputy Judge Advocate.

1. The Commander of the Forces has been much concerned to receive reports of the misconduct of the soldiers left behind, in all the hospitals, particularly at Oporto; and he desires that in future, whenever an hospital is established, the following Regulations will be observed:

" When soldiers are dismissed from the hospital as convalescents, they are, if possible, to be quartered in the same building; if that should not be possible, they are to be quartered on the inhabitants of the house in which the

hospital

(68)

hospital is established; in either case the Officers in charge of the men left behind in hospital are to attend, and to put in execution the Orders of the 29th ult. relative to visiting the soldiers in their quarters.

" 2. No convalescent must ever be permitted to appear out of his quarters in the streets of the town, excepting with his side arms, and dressed according to the orders of his regiment. As soon as a sufficient number of convalescents are strong enough, a guard must be mounted daily, of which patroles under a Non-commissioned Officer must be sent during the night to take up all soldiers straggling from their quarters after hours. Convalescents must parade with their arms twice a day, once in the morning, and in the evening at sun-set; all Officers being present at each parade. After the evening parade, the soldiers are to be marched to their quarters, and none are to be permitted to appear in the streets after that hour.

" 3. All Officers left in sick quarters, in any town where an hospital is established, are to be considered as belonging to the hospital until they shall have recovered, and are to do duty according to their respective ranks with the Officers left in charge of the sick men in hospital, till they shall be ordered to join the army.

" 4. The Officer commanding at each of the hospitals, including that of Lisbon, will report to the Adjutant General that these orders have been carried into execution, along with the weekly report ordered to be made by the General Orders of the 13th June. Copies of these orders are to be sent to all the hospitals, and a copy to be left by the Adjutant General wherever an hospital may be left in future.

" 5. When

" 5. When the army, or any portion of it, in future requires green forage, Commissaries, or if there should be no Commissary, the Quarter-Master of the regiment, under the orders of the General or Commanding Officer, will make a requisition upon the magistrate for it, and will point out to him the field or place from whence it can be provided: the magistrate is then to have it cut; forage is to be delivered to the troops by the Commissary, in rations, according to the ordered proportions. A guard will be left in the field, in charge of the remainder of the forage, after the Commissary has made his delivery. If there should be no magistrate, or if the magistrate should refuse to consent to deliver or cut the green forage, or if it should be necessary on any account the troops should cut it for themselves, the Commissary of the brigade or regiment, accompanied by an Officer of the Quarter-Master General's department, or if there should be none with that division of troops, by the Quarter-Master of a regiment, and if possible by the magistrate of the place, or the occupier of the ground, or by some inhabitant of the country, is to proceed to value the field, and to estimate the number of rations of forage it contains. Having done this, the Commissary is to allot the field in its due proportions to the Quarter-Masters of the different regiments to be supplied with forage from it; parties of fatigue from those regiments, under the command of an Officer, are to proceed and cut and carry away the forage thus allotted to them. For all green forage required, the usual receipts must be given.

" 6. The Commissary of each division, brigade, or re-, giment, on his arrival in any place near which he understands the troops to which he is attached are to halt more

than

than one night, must take immediate and effectual measures to ascertain the number of ovens in the neighbourhood; and if they should be insufficient to supply the troops to which he is attached with bread, he will take care that a sufficient number are built forthwith.

" 8. No man of the brigades in huts must be allowed to quit the lines of his regiment without being dressed with his side arms, according to the orders of his regiment."

ADJUTANT GENERAL'S OFFICE.
Abrantes, 18th *June,* 1809.

G. O.

1. WHEN the Commissary issues English hay, the ration is to be 10 lbs. for each horse or mule; when he issues straw, or any other forage of the country, it is to be 14 lbs.

2. The Commander of the Forces is concerned, from reports which have been lately made to him of the practice of some of the regiments in the army, to be obliged to desire the Captains of companies to inspect the arms, ammunition, and flints, in possession of the soldiers of their companies at every parade with arms, and particularly on the march, which takes place on the morning of a march.

3. Colonel Low, of the King's German Legion, is appointed to act as Brigadier General till his Majesty's pleasure is known, and is to command the brigade of the Legion, consisting of the 5th and 7th battalions of the line.

Brigadier

Brigadier General Low will be pleased to recommend an Officer as his Brigade Major.

4. As the weather will now admit of the troops hutting, and they can therefore move together in large bodies, brigades are to be formed into divisions as follows :

Guards . . . .
Brig. Gen. Cameron's Brigade . . . } 1st Division.
Hanoverian Legion . . . .

Major Gen. Hill's Brigade . . . . } 2d Division.
Brig. Gen. R. Stewart's ditto . . . .

Major Gen. M'Kenzie's Brigade . . } 3d Division.
Colonel Donkin's ditto . . . . . .

Brig. Gen. A. Campbell's Brigade . . } 4th Division.
Colonel Peacocke's ditto . . . . .

Lieutenant General Sherbrooke will take the command of the 1st division; the senior General Officers of brigades will respectively take the command of the division in which their brigades are placed, till the other Lieutenant Generals will join the army.

The brigades in divisions are to be formed from the right, as placed in this order :

The divisions will stand in one or more lines, in respect to each other, as will be ordered at the time.

An Assistant Adjutant General will be attached to the Officer commanding the division; an Assistant Provost will also be attached to each division.

Assistant Adjutant Generals are attached as follows :

Lieutenant Colonel Lord Aylmer, 1st Division.
Captain Cotton . . . . 2d ditto.
Major Williamson . . . . . . 3d ditto.
Captain Cooke . . . . 4th ditto.

5. The

5. The General Court Martial assembled at Barquintia, of which Brigadier General Langworth was president, is dissolved.

6. As soon as the horses lately brought from England by the Royal Waggon Train, are delivered over to the artillery, all the drivers of the Royal Waggon Train are to be sent to join their troops at Santarem.

The Officers and men are to be under the directions of the Commissary General, who will receive his orders from the Commander of the Forces, respecting their future disposal; in the mean time the detachment at Lisbon is to be completed to one troop, from Santarem, in order to take charge of the Irish Commissariat horses at that place.

7. The following Serjeants are appointed Assistant Provost Marshals to the army, from the date hereof:

Serjeant Webster Boyle, Fuzileers, to be attached to the 4th division; Serjeant Lightbody, 50th Foot; Serjeant Xenophon Mosscroft, 48th Foot. They will attend to-morrow morning at 10 o'clock, at the Adjutant General's Office, for orders.

ADJUTANT GENERAL'S OFFICE.
Abrantes, 19th June, 1809.

G. O.

1. THE following articles and necessaries, belonging to the Non-commissioned Officers and soldiers of the 3d Dragoon Guards and 4th Dragoons, are to be left behind :—One horse cloth, a snaffle bridle, one shirt, one pair of stockings, one pair of shoes, one pair of breeches, a curry comb and brush, two shoe brushes, gaiters : the
articles

articles belonging to each dragoon are to be put up separately in their horse sheet, and the men's name marked upon the bundle; the whole are then to be made up in such parcels as will be convenient for removal, marking each with the number; and these are to be lodged in the Commissaries' stores at Abrantes, taking the company's receipt for the number of parcels.

The Officers commanding regiments will take care to keep with the regiments a list of the names of the soldiers who leave their necessaries behind under this order.

2. The Commissary General will take care that all regimental baggage and stores lodged in the stores at Abrantes, for which he will give his receipt, are sent to Lisbon by water, and lodged in the regimental stores of the regiment to which it belongs; and his Officers at Lisbon will take the receipt of the Non-commissioned in charge of the regimental stores at Lisbon, for it.

3. Mr. Deputy Commissary Melville is directed to put himself under the orders of Marshal Beresford.

4. The Honourable Leslie Melville and James Roper Head, Esqrs. are appointed to act as Assistant Commissaries, and are to place themselves under the orders of Marshal Beresford.

5. There are so many complaints and references respecting the mules attached to regiments, that it is necessary again to state in orders the principles on which they are given.

Each regiment of Infantry, consisting of 10 companies, has 15 mules, of which one for each company is allotted to carry the company's camp kettles, one to carry the Surgeon's instruments, and one to carry the Paymaster's books. Captains of companies, Paymasters, and

Surgeons,

Surgeons, each of whom has received 10*l.* bât money, and is bound to keep up those mules, which were originally given to them by the Commissariat, as a matter of favour by the late Commander of the 'Forces. One mule is attached to each regiment of Infantry to carry the intrenching tools, and is, by different orders, to be in charge of the Quarter-Masters of regiments.

The Commander of the Forces desires that the Commissaries in each brigade will see the intrenching tool mules in charge of each brigade this afternoon, and that they will hereafter see them once a week.

The mules allotted for the carriage of intrenching tools, are the public property, and must be kept up at the public charge.

Each regiment of Cavalry has 14 mules, 8 for carrying camp kettles, one for the Surgeon, one for the Paymaster, respectively, having received bât money for, and liable to keep up; besides these, a regiment of Cavalry has one mule for the Veterinary Surgeon, one for the Serjeant Armourer, one for the Serjeant Saddler, and one for the intrenching tools.

These four last are the property of the public, and must be kept up at the public expence; they must be taken care of by the persons for whose use they are provided, respectively; and the Commanding Officers of regiments will give directions that one of the Quarter-Masters may take charge of the mule for the intrenching tools. The Assistant Commissaries, with regiments of Cavalry, will see these public mules attached to regiments of Cavalry this afternoon; and in future they will inspect them once a week.

Commanding Officers of regiments of Cavalry and
Infantry

Infantry are requested to give particular directions to the Quarter-Masters, and others in charge of the public mules, to take the greatest care of. them, and to see that they are applied to no other use than that for which they are allowed; as in many instances the Commissary was under the necessity of supplying the regiments with hired mules to carry camp kettles, Surgeons chests, and Paymasters books, of which the public have been paying the hire ever since. The Commissary General is requested, as soon as possible, to supply the Officers with purchased instead of hired mules.

6. The Captains, Surgeons, and Paymasters of regiments, which have lately arrived, or may hereafter arrive, in Portugal, from Great Britain or Ireland, or the islands, and which have received the allowance called embarkation money, are to provide themselves with mules, for the carriage of camp kettles, Paymasters' books, or Surgeons' chests, respectively; and the Captains, Paymasters, and Surgeons of those regiments, which arrived from Gibraltar, and have not received the allowance called Embarkation Money, will be allowed each 20*l.* to purchase a mule for their service.

7. Mr. Joseph Peter Sullivan is attached to the corps of Guides, with the pay and allowances of Cornet, from the 1st June inclusive.

G. O.

ADJUTANT GENERAL's OFFICE.
Abrantes, 20th June, 1809.

1. WHEN the troops march with a route, it must be invariably specified, in the route, where they are to get provisions;

provisions; and they are to receive provisions according to what is stated in the route. The Commissaries attached to brigades and regiments of Cavalry, must not issue provisions to troops marching with a route, unless it is specified in the route that they are to do so.

2. As the supply of cattle is not now plenty, all the troops in the huts, and towns of Abrantes and Punhite, and the neighbouring cantonments, will be supplied with salt meat for a few days.

4. The Assistant Provost Marshals are to be kept on the strength of their regiments, and returned on command; Brigadier General R. Stewart's brigade will furnish the public duties to-morrow.

G. O.

Adjutant General's Office.
Abrantes, 21st June, 1809.

1. Commanding Officers of regiments will order all Officers on leave of absence at Lisbon to join the army forthwith.

2. The Paymasters of regiments will receive from the Paymaster General the balances due on their respective estimates, from 25th April to 24th May; the corps at and near Abrantes this afternoon; those at Punhite, Tancos, Barquintia, and Thomar, to-morrow; General M'Kenzie's and Colonel Donkin's brigades the day after to-morrow: the corps will at the same time and place receive from the Commissary General the shoes for which they have made a requisition on the Commissary General, under the orders of the 8th instant.

3. The Commissary General will on the day after to-

morrow

morrow furnish the Paymaster General with an account of shirts issued to the different corps, in order that they may be charged against them, in the discharge of the estimates, from 25th May to 14th June.

4. The 20th Light Dragoons having arrived at Lisbon, this corps is to embark, with all their horses, as soon as transports shall be prepared for their reception ; all order-lies and dismounted men belonging to the 20th, are to proceed to Lisbon to join their corps as soon as possible. The Commander of the Forces cannot part with the detachment of the 20th Light Dragoons under the command of Major Blake, which has been serving with this army, without expressing his approbation of their conduct, and his acknowledgment of their services. They are separated from this army solely that they may join the remainder of the regiment, and may have more extensive opportunities of distinguishing themselves; and wherever they will serve, they will have the anxious wishes of the Commander of the Forces for their success.

5. At a General Court Martial held at Barquintia on the 15th of June, by order of his Excellency Lieutenant General Sir Arthur Wellesley, of which Brigadier General E. Langworth was President, the following prisoners, Gunner George Schlothawer, Gunner Henry Bowle, and Condridge Statze, driver of the German Royal Artillery, were tried for disorderly and unsoldier-like conduct, committed in a small private chapel near Coimbra, on or about the 16th ult. and on suspicion of taking from thence several articles, which were found in their haversacks and knapsacks.

The Court having fully and maturely weighed the evidence against the prisoners, as well as what they had to

offer

offer in their defence, were of opinion that the prisoners, Gunner George Schlothawer and Driver Condridge Stratze, were guilty of the crime laid to their charge, a breach of the Articles of War; but that the prisoner Henry Bowle is not guilty, and do therefore acquit him. The Court having found the prisoners, George Schlothawer and Condridge Statze, guilty, sentence George Schlothawer to receive 800 *lashes*, and Statze 100 *lashes*, in the usual manner, at such time and place as his Excellency shall be pleased to appoint; which sentence the Commander of the Forces has confirmed, and directs the same to be carried into execution against Schlothawer at six o'clock this evening, in presence of the Royal German Artillery; but, in consequence of a letter received from the President, containing a recommendation of Driver Condridge Statze, the Commander of the Forces is pleased to remit his sentence.

6. The General Hospital at the Convent of St. Antonio at Abrantes, being now ready for the reception of sick, the Surgeons of regiments may send such of their patients there as are not likely to do well in cantonments; but they are previously to be inspected by the Staff Surgeons of the divisions, as none can be received into the General Hospital without his approving signature.

7. Captain Mellish, Deputy A. A. General, is attached to the 4th division of the army till the arrival of Captain Cooke, detained by sickness at Lisbon.

ADJU-

ADJUTANT GENERAL's OFFICE.

G. O.   *22d June,* 1809.

2. COLONEL PEACOCKE, Coldstream Guards, will command the British troops in garrison at Lisbon.

His Majesty has been pleased to appoint Colonel Anson, 16th Dragoons, to be a Brigadier General on the Staff of this army, from 25th May.

Brigadier General Anson is to command the brigade lately commanded by Colonel Peacocke.

3. Serjeant James Duval, of the 4th Dragoons, is appointed an Assistant Provost Marshal from the date hereof, and is to be attached to the division of Cavalry. Assistant Provost Lightbody is attached to the 1st division of the army.

ADJUTANT GENERAL's OFFICE.

G. O.   *Abrantes, 23d June,* 1809.

3. THE Paymasters of regiments who have not already received it, are to receive 10*l.* bat money, in the same manner as Surgeons of regiments, under the orders of the 19th instant (paragraph 5.)

4. Deputy Assistant Adjutant General, Deputy Assistant Quarter-Master General, Majors of brigade, and Aides-de-Camps, will be allowed forage for three horses and one mule from the date hereof.

ADJU-

ADJUTANT GENERAL'S OFFICE.
Abrantes, 23d June, 1809.

A. G. O.

MAJOR General Hill will command the second division of infantry until further orders.

Major General Tilson will join and command the brigade of Infantry hitherto commanded by Major General Hill.

ADJUTANT GENERAL'S OFFICE.
Abrantes, 24*th June,* 1809.

G. O.

1. THE frequent irregularities which occur on the march of detachments of convalescents, or recruits to join their regiments with the army, render it necessary to publish the following regulations :

2. All detachments must march by a route from the Quarter-Master General's department, in which they will be named, the places at which such detachments will receive provisions, and from whom.

3. The Commanding Officer of each detachment on its march, must take care to send forward notice to the person from whom the provisions are to be received, of the arrival of the detachment, and of its strength.

4. It is to be understood that when two or more days provisions are issued to the troops, they are not to receive at the same time, two or more days wine. It has already been frequently explained in orders, that wine forms no part of the soldier's ration, it will be delivered to them when it

can

can be procured, and when it cannot they must go without it.

5. When a detachment will move, the soldiers must be
formed into divisions, and Officers and Non-commissioned
Officers must be posted to each division.

The orders of the 29th May must be particularly attended to by the Officers posted to divisions; and they
must exert themselves to prevent the repetition of the
complaints which are so disgraceful to the army.

6. A detachment must universally march at day light
in the morning, the Officers and Non-commissioned Officers must march with the divisions, to which they are
posted, and must prevent the soldiers falling out of the
ranks and straggling. The detachments must march at
the rate of two miles and a half an hour, one halt must
be made for five or ten minutes at the end of every hour
and a half.

7. Officers commanding detachments are to report their
progress to head quarters by every opportunity.

8. A communication between head quarters and all
parts of Portugal is to be carried on through Lisbon: all
Officers, having occasion to write, must send their letters
by post, under cover, unless specially ordered to do otherwise to the Town Major, Lisbon, from whose office
a courier will be dispatched daily to head quarters.

9. Whenever an Officer is sent from any of the hospitals, or Lisbon, in the command of a detachment of
convalescents or recruits, he is to be furnished with a copy
of these orders, and on his arrival at head quarters, he
will report specially that the orders in the 3d, 5th, and
6th articles of this day's orders have been carried into
effect.

10. The number of horses, for which Staff Officers are allowed to draw forage, having been encreased by the orders of the 23d instant, it is to be understood that they are to do all duties required from them by means of their own horses, unless when required to go and return from a place at a greater distance from their station than 20 miles.

11. At a General Court Martial, held by order of his Excellency Lieutenant General Sir Arthur Wellesley, K. B. Commander of the Forces, on the 16th June, and continued by adjournments, of which Brigadier General A. Campbell was President, and Captain S. B. Achmuty, 7th Foot, was Deputy Judge Advocate; the Court proceeded to the trial of private William Green, of the 66th Regiment, for unsoldier-like conduct, and insolence, in using disrespectful language, threatening and striking Ensign Fox, when ordered to be taken to the guard-house by him, on the evening of the 13th April, 1809; and the Court having maturely weighed and considered the evidence against the prisoner, together with what he has urged in his defence, is of opinion, that he, the said William Green, is guilty of the first part of the charge, viz. in using disrespectful language to Ensign Fox, 66th Foot, which being a breach of the Articles of War, do sentence him to receive 500 lashes, in such manner, and at such time and place as his Excellency the Commander of the Forces shall direct. The Court was of opinion, that the prisoner, William Green, was not guilty of the 2d and 3d parts of the charge, namely in threatening and striking Ensign Fox, and do therefore acquit him thereof; which sentence has been confirmed by his Excellency the Commander of the Forces.

12. The

12. The Court next proceeded to the trial of George Best, George Marshall, John Thomas, and James Summers, privates of the 2d Regiment, for being concerned in plundering, on the evening of the 12th June, 1809; and the Court having maturely weighed and considered the evidence against the prisoners, together with what they had to allege in their defence, was of opinion, that the prisoners, George Best, George Marshall, and John Thomas, were guilty of the crime laid to their charge, namely, being concerned in plundering, on the 12th June, 1809; and do therefore sentence them, the said George Best, George Marshall, and John Thomas, to receive 500 lashes each, in such manner and at such time and place as his Excellency the Commander of the Forces shall direct.

The Court is of opinion that the prisoner, James Summers, is not guilty of the crime laid to his charge, and do therefore acquit him thereof.

13. The Court next proceeded to the trial of James Muller, private in the 71st Regiment, for unsoldier-like conduct, in attempting to break open a door near Captain Cameron's quarters, of the 3d Regiment.

The Court having maturely weighed and considered the evidence against the prisoner, together with what he has alleged in his defence, was of opinion that he was not guilty of the crime laid to his charge, as he was using means which he thought justifiable to get into the billet, and do therefore acquit him thereof; which sentence has been confirmed by his Excellency the Commander of the Forces.

James Summers of the 2d Regiment, and James Mul-

ler

ler of the 71st are released, and will join their regiments forthwith.

14. The 1st and 2d battalions detachments, the 66th, and one company from each of the other regiments in camp, are to parade this evening at six o'clock in front of the 2d division of infantry in camp, under the orders of Major General Tilson, in order to witness the execution of the sentence of the General Court Martial.

First Lieutenant Joda Carlos de Tamm of the Portuguese Engineers, is attached to the Quarter-Master General's department, with the pay and allowances of Deputy Assistant Quarter-Master General, from the 25th May.

G. O.

ADJUTANT GENERAL's OFFICE.
Abrantes, 25th June, 1809.

2. PAYMASTERS of regiments at Abrantes and in the huts, and all Officers of the army, or others to whom any money is due, whether on account of claims for losses, which claims have been before the Board of Claims, for horses shot for the glanders, or on any other account, are to call on the Paymaster General this afternoon, where the former will receive payment for the subsistence of their respective regiments to the 24th June, and all the latter what may be due to them.

3. Paymasters of regiments and all persons to whom money may be due, stationed at Punhete, Thomar, Taucos, Barquintia, and Atalayo, are to wait upon the Paymaster General to-morrow, when they will receive payment in like manner; Paymasters of regiments in General

M'Ken-

M'Kenzie's division will receive payment when they bring their estimates.

4. The accounts of the soldiers of the army to the 24th June, must be settled and signed, and balances paid on this day and to-morrow, and those in camp ; to those at a distance on the following days. General Officers commanding brigades are requested to see this order carried into execution.

5. The army will march on Tuesday and following days, according to routes which the Quarter-Master General will send.

6. To-morrow the troops in camp are to receive biscuit for four days, viz. 27th, 28th, 29th, and 30th, inclusive. Commissaries of brigades or regiments will apprize the Commanding Officers of the regiments to which they are attached, where the bread is to be received. The troops in General Sherbrook's division, and General Cotton's Brigade of Cavalry, will receive directions from the Quarter Master General respecting the receipt of their bread.

7. The troops in the huts are this day to apply to the Quarter-Master General for orders on the Commissary General's Stores, for the camp kettles, canteens, haversacks, and bill-hooks, for which they have made requisitions under the orders of the 8th instant ; General Sherbrook's division will receive the same articles as they will pass through Abrantes on the 27th ; the same articles will be sent to General Cotton's brigade, and the infantry of Major General M'Kenzie's division.

8. The allowance of intrenching tools is to be only five spades, five shovels, five pick-axes, and five felling axes, for each battalion of infantry ; eight spades, eight shovels,

four

four pick axes, and four felling axes for each regiment of Cavalry; and the requisitions will be corrected accordingly.

9. The Deputy Inspector of Hospitals will give directions for the formation of the hospitals at Abrantes, upon the principle, that all the men likely to continue sick for any length of time, are to go to a General Hospital, which is to be formed under the care of a sufficient number of Surgeons of each brigade. All the sick, excepting those of Major General M'Kenzie's division, in the huts, or at Abrantes, are to be at Abrantes; and the General Officers commanding brigades, are to take measures to send the sick of their brigades to Abrantes as soon as possible.

10. The Commander of the Forces is under the necessity of again requesting the attention of all the Officers of the Army, to the strict obedience of the orders issued, particularly to those respecting supplies of provisions, carts, boats, &c. It is again positively forbid to any Officer to stop supplies going to any part of the army, or to press boats, or carriages, excepting under the directions of a Commissary. The Commissariat Drivers attached to the Artillery at Abrantes, and all the other stations of the army, must this day be delivered over to the Commissary General or his Assistants.

ADJUTANT GENERAL's OFFICE.
Abrantes, 26th June, 1810.

G. O.

1. THE Commander of the Forces desires that the troops should always march at day-light, in order that they may reach the ground at as early an hour as may be practicable;

practicable; he is also desirous that they should hut every day; and it is to be understood that they are to hut invariably where there is wood conveniently situated, in reference to water. This wood however, must not be olive trees, or other valuable fruit trees.

2. The Order (No. 5 of the 3d May) in respect to men taken sick on the march, referring to the order (No. 11 of the 24th April) by the late Commander of the Forces, is countermanded. The Commander of the Forces being convinced, that from circumstances, it is impossible to carry it into execution.

3. In future, the General Officers commanding divisions and brigades will direct, that men taken sick upon a march, may be carried on till orders will be given for forming a general or brigade hospital.

4. The huts at present occupied by Major General Tilson's brigade, are to be occupied as hospitals by the sick of the different regiments to be left in brigade hospital.

5. The Staff Surgeons attached to divisions will make the distribution of the huts to the different brigades, and will order a sufficient number of Surgeons from each brigade, to remain in the huts to attend the sick. This order is not to prevent the Surgeons of those brigades which have already got hospitals in the town of Abrantes from continuing to occupy them. Surgeons of regiments are to make requisitions on the Purveyor's Stores for bedding for the sick, in the proportion of a blanket for every patient in the huts.

6. A sufficient number of Officers and Non-commissioned Officers from each brigade are to be left in charge

of

of the sick at Abrantes, according to the orders of the 19th of May and 2d of June.

7. The Officers commanding companies are at all times to leave with the Surgeons in charge of hospitals in which the men are left, the amount of the hospital stoppages of 9d. per diem for each man left behind, from the day the men will enter the hospital to the following 24th of the month, as soon as possible after the 24th of every month. The Surgeons in charge of hospitals, are invariably to send to the Paymasters of regiments, by the mode of conveyance pointed out in the orders of the 24th instant, the account of stoppages for the men of each regiment who have been in the hospital under their charge since the 24th of the preceding month, according to the printed form—no accounts of stoppages must be sent to England in future.

8. A few tents having arrived, those Officers who have made known their wishes to have them under the orders of the 24th May, No. 3, are to apply to the Quarter-Master General, who will give orders upon the Commissary General for them.

9. Complaints having been made by the Lieutenant General commanding the cavalry, by Brigadier General Fane, and by Lieutenant Colonel Lord Edward Somerset, commanding the 4th Dragoons, to which regiment Mr. Assistant Commissary Gordon is attached, of his neglect of duty, of incapacity to perform his duty, and of his making false reports to Lieutenant Colonel Lord Edward Somerset; Mr. Assistant Commissary Gordon is dismissed from his Office as Assistant Commissary. Mr. Gordon is to be released from arrest, and is to quit the army.

10. The

10. The Paymaster of the 1st battalion detachments being sick, the Officers commanding that battalion will appoint the usual Committee, according to his Majesty's Regulations, to take charge, and to do the duty of the office of Paymaster.

12. A Brigade Court Martial held at Castello Branco, on the 19th June, by order of Colonel Donkin, of which Captain Andrews of the 60th regiment was President, proceeded to the trial of Patrick Magher, 60th regiment, for unsoldierlike conduct. The Court having considered the evidence against the prisoner, together with what he had to offer in his defence, are of opinion, he was guilty of the crime laid to his charge, viz. a breach of the Articles of War; and therefore sentence him, the said private Patrick Magher, to receive 900 lashes, at such time and place as the Officer commanding shall think fit; which sentence was approved of by his Excellency the Commander of the Forces.

13. The Deputy Paymaster General will, to-morrow morning, advance to the General and Staff Officers who have demands upon Mr. Deputy Paymaster Hunter, upon a warrant of the late Commander of the Forces for the Staff Pay in advance to the 24th June, such sums on account of Mr. Deputy Paymaster General Hunter, as may appear to be due to those Officers respectively. Mr. Deputy Paymaster Hunter will settle these accounts with Mr. Boys forthwith.

ADJUTANT GENERAL'S OFFICE.

G. A. O.　　　　*Abrantes, 26th June,* 1809.

THE General Court Martial of which Brigadier General

neral

neral A. Campbell is President, having assembled on the
7th instant pursuant to adjournment, proceeded to the
trial of Private Robert Langton, 40th regiment, tried
upon the following charges, (viz.)

For being absent from his regiment and for being concerned in coining, and having instruments for coining in
his possession.

The Court having maturely weighed and considered the
evidence against the prisoner, Robert Langton, of the
40th regiment, together with what he has alleged in his
defence, is of opinion that he is guilty of the first and
third counts of the charge, namely, being absent from
his regiment, and having instruments for coining found in
his possession, in breach of the Articles of War, and does
therefore sentence him the said Robert Langton, 40th regiment, to receive 600 lashes, in such manner and at
such time and place as His Excellency the Commander
of the Forces may think proper to appoint.

The Court is of opinion that the prisoner Robert Langton, 40th regiment, is not guilty of the second count,
namely, being concerned in coining, and do therefore acquit him thereof.

His Excellency the Commander of the Forces has been
pleased to approve the foregoing sentence, and directs,
that a company of each regiment in the huts is to parade
this evening in front of Major-General Tilson's brigade,
the whole under the command of a Field Officer, to witness the execution of the sentence of the Court Martial
on private Robert Langton.

The General Court Martial of which Brigadier General
A. Campbell is President, is dissolved.

Captain

Captain Raymond Pelly, of the 16th Light Dragoons, is apointed Aide-de-Camp to Brigadier General Anson.

Brigadier Major Fordyce will continue to do duty with Major General Hill, and will act as the Deputy Assistant General with his division till further orders.

Major-General Tilson will make an arrangement for doing the duty of Brigade-Major of his brigade till further orders.

———

Adjutant General's Office.
Abrantes, 27th June, 1809.

G. O.

1. Lieutenant Wurmb, 5th line battalion King's German Legion, is appointed Aid de Camp to Brigadier General Low till His Majesty's pleasure is known; Captain Backmaister, 5th line battalion King's German Legion, is to act as Brigade-Major to the 2d battalion King's German Legion till His Majesty's pleasure is known.

2. Seven horses of the 3d Dragoon Guards, three horses of the 4th Dragoons, reported by Lieutenant General Payne unfit for service, are to be cast and sold this evening at 6 o'clock, in the cavalry lines, under the direction of the Assistant Commissary attached to the 3d Dragoon Guards.

3. The Paymaster General will make advances to the Paymasters of those regiments which have given in their estimates to the 24th July, not exceeding one third of the amount of each estimate.

A Guard of one Serjeant and six Dragoons from Brigadier General Fane's brigade to be attached to the Paymaster General's mules during the march; they are to report

port themselves and receive instructions from the Paymaster General, one Corporal and two private Dragoons to be attached to the Provost Guard, which, with all the prisoners, will move with the head quarters of the army.

7. The King's German Legion have disobeyed the repeated orders to leave Officers at Coimbra in charge of their sick.

8. At a General Court Martial held at Abrantes, by order of His Excellency Lieutenant General Sir A. Wellesley, K. B. at which Brigadier General A. Campbell was President, and Major Achmuty Deputy Judge-Advocate, on the 26th instant: The Court proceeded to the trial of Edward Scraugh, of the 7th line battalion King's German Legion, for having deserted from his battalion. The Court having maturely weighed and considered the evidence against the prisoner, together with what he alleged in his defence, was of opinion that he was guilty of the crime laid to his charge, in breach of the articles of war, and therefore sentence him, the said Edward Scraugh of the King's German Legion, to receive 600 lashes, in such manner and at such time and place as His Excellency the Commander of the Forces shall think fit to appoint: which sentence, Lieutenant General Sir Arthur Wellesley has confirmed. The King's German Legion will parade this evening, in front of the lines, at 6 o'clock, under the direction of the General Officer commanding, in order to see the above sentence carried into execution.

9. Mr. J. Bollemat is attached to the Quarter-Master General's Department from 25th April, to be employed in the Drawing Room, with an allowance of one dollar and a half per diem and one ration.

10. Mr.

10. Mr. Assistant Commissary Gordon having expressed his concern for the neglect of duty of which he has been guilty, and Lieutenant General Payne having expressed a desire his conduct should be looked over upon this occasion, and that he should be reinstated in his office; the order of yesterday respecting him is countermanded, and he is to return to his duty as Assistant Commissary attached to the 4th Dragoons.

The Commander of the Forces, however, hopes Mr. Gordon will shew by his attention to his duty in future, that he merits the indulgence of Lieutenant General Payne; and he hopes that the example of the dismissal of Mr. Gordon for the neglect of duty, will operate as an example to all the Officers of the Commissariat.

ADJUTANT GENERAL's OFFICE.
G. O.   *Castello Branca*, *1st July* 1810.

1. MAJOR General Hills, and the 4th division of Infantry and the heavy six-pounder brigade of Artillery, are to march to-morrow morning at 4 o'clock, according to routes from the Quarter-Master General; these troops are this day to receive bread for the 3d and 4th inclusive: such men belonging to these divisions as are unable to march on account of sickness, must be left in the hospital at Castello Branca, under charge of Officers and Non-Commissioned Officers according to the proportion of the General Orders (19th May, No. 3.); subsistence at 9d. per diem to the 24th July is to be left with them.

2. Great care must be taken when rye is given to the horses that they are not watered two hours before, or two

hours

hours after they are fed; the same rule should be observed when they are fed with Indian corn or barley.

ADJUTANT GENERAL'S OFFICE.

Castello Branca, 1st July, 1809.

A. G. O.

CAPTAIN A. Campbell, Aide-de-Camp to Brigadier General Campbell, is appointed to act as Deputy Assistant with the Adjutant General's Department.

Assistant Surgeon M'Gelivray, 14th Light Dragoons, to act as Surgeon to the 5th battalion 60th regiment, till His Majesty's pleasure is known.

ADJUTANT GENERAL'S OFFICE.

Zarza Mayor, 4th July, 1809.

G. O.

1. THE Assistant Adjutant Generals, and Brigade Majors of those divisions and brigades stationed in the neighbourhood of Head Quarters, must attend at the Adjutant General's Office for orders, at 10 o'clock precisely.

2. The Brigade Majors will attend at the Assistant Adjutant Generals of divisions to receive the division orders, at half past 11 o'clock, and at one the Brigade Majors must give out the orders to the Adjutants of regiments, which must be given out to troops and companies, and read to the soldiers at evening parades.

3. In case circumstances should prevent the Brigade Majors from issuing the General Orders to the Adjutants of regiments before 3 o'clock on any halting day, they are to receive and issue on that day only the orders requiring im-

mediate

mediate execution, of which the General Officers commanding brigades are to make the selection, and on the following day the other orders of General Regulations.

4. All orders received by the Adjutants of regiments must at the first parade, or earlier if necessary, be read to the troops.

5. On marching days the Assistant Adjutant Generals, and Brigade Majors stationed near head quarters will attend at the Adjutant General's Office for orders, as soon as the troops reach their ground.

6. All orders requiring immediate execution issued on marching days must be given to the Adjutants, and read to the troops as soon as possible.

7. The General Orders will be sent from head quarters to divisions at a distance by the first opportunity, those requiring immediate execution must be issued and read to the troops as soon as received; the others, if not received by the General Officer of the division before two P. M. are not to be issued till the following day.

8. The Assistant Adjutant Generals, or the Brigade Major of the division or brigade at a distance to which the General Orders will have been sent, must send to the Adjutant General by the first opportunity, a receipt for the orders received, specifying the numbers of each day.

9. When Pass Orders will be sent, directions will be written on the back of them, stating whether they are to be circulated by the person who will have carried them from Head Quarters, or to the Officers respectively to whom they will have been addressed.

10. Every Officer to whom they are addressed must sign his name on the paper on receiving them, and insert the hour of the day at which they reached him.

11. As

11. As Pass Orders invariably must require immediate execution, they must be issued and read to the troops without loss of time.

12. The numberless mistakes which have occurred, and the many instances of neglect and disobedience of orders issued referring to the health, subsistence, or the convenience of the troops, renders it necessary not only to observe the early circulation of orders, but if possible, obedience to them and their early and prompt execution.

13. The obedience to orders of General Regulations must depend upon the attention of General Officers commanding brigades, and Commanding Officers of regiments, and their determination to enforce regularity and discipline, but obedience to them requiring execution can be secured by other means.

14. Accordingly the Commander of the Forces desires that Officers commanding regiments shall report to the General Officer commanding the brigade, that the General Orders requiring the performance of any duty, or the execution of any arrangement have been obeyed.

15. The General Officers commanding divisions and brigades will take care to notify to the troops, to what day they have received bread upon every issue. The regiments of Major General M'Kenzie's brigade, and the 1st Hussars, have received bread to the 4th July inclusive.

16. The Guards furnished by General M'Kenzie's brigade are to be relieved this evening, at sunset, by Major General Hill's division.

17. The Commander of the Forces requests the attention of General Officers commanding divisions and brigades to the General Orders of the 4th and 5th March, by the late Commander of the Forces, relative to the use of the

mules

mules allowed for carrying camp kettles, in any service excepting the carriage of camp kettles.

18. The consequence of loading them with other baggage is, that they are unequal to carry the kettles which they are given to convey, and the loads are so ill put on that they fall from the mules, and the camp kettles do not arrive from the march till after the hour at which they ought to be used by the troops.

20. General Staff and other Officers are requested to put their names on the doors of the houses in which they are quartered.

G. O.
ADJUTANT GENERAL's OFFICE.
Zarza Mayor, 5th July, 1809.

1. THE Commander of the Forces desires that it may be considered as a standing order, that the troops are not to quit their lines, unless dressed according to the orders of their regiment, with their side arms; excepting when on fatigue duty, in which case they must be in charge of an Officer, or Non-commissioned Officer according to their numbers.

G. A. O.
ADJUTANT GENERAL's OFFICE.
5th July, 1809.

Rev. James Alliot is appointed a Chaplain to the Forces, to bear date from the 1st May.

Rev. H. S. Seymour is appointed a Chaplain to the Forces, appointment dated as above.

ADJUTANT GENERAL'S OFFICE.

GENERAL PASS ORDER,   *5th July*, 1809.

CAPTAIN Dunbar, of the 66th regiment, is appointed to act as Brigade Major to Major General Tilson's brigade till further orders.

Captain George Munroe is appointed Aide de Camp to Lieutenant General Sherbrooke, from the 25th June.

ADJUTANT GENERAL'S OFFICE.
Placencia, 9*th July*, 1809.

G. O.

1. ALL the Officers belonging to regiments which are in huts, must be encamped with the men, excepting those whose health requires that they should remain in houses: applications for quarters for those Officers must be made through the General Officer commanding the brigade, to the Officer of the Quarter-Master General's department with the division, or with Head Quarters.

2. The Officer of the Quarter-Master General's department with divisions, must quarter the General Officers and their Staff as near to their divisions and brigades as possible.

3. All Officers, whether of the Staff or Regiments, requiring quarters at Head Quarters, must apply to Captain Kelly of the Quarter-Master General's department; and all Officers requiring quarters at the Head Quarters of any division must apply to the Quarter-Master General of the division.

No Officer, excepting those of the department of the Quarter-Master General, employed in this branch of the service, must apply for quarters to the magistrates.

.. 4. As

4. As Commissaries have been appointed to supply all and every part of the army, to whom every individual, entitled to provisions and forage, can apply for what he requires, no application, excepting by the Commissaries, must be made by any Officer, or Soldier, or other persons attached to the army, to the magistrates of the country for any article whatever.

5. A General Court Martial will assemble to-morrow morning, at 11 o'clock, for the trial of such prisoners as will be brought before it.

Major General M'Kenzie, President.

	Field Officers.	Captains.	Subalterns.
Major Gen. M'Kenzie's Brigade .	1	2	1
Major General Hill's Division . .	2	1	2
Brigadier Gen. Campbell's do. .	1	3	1
Total . .	4	6	4

The name of the Officer apppointed to act as Deputy Judge Advocate will be sent in the course of the day to the President.

All evidences to proceed immediately to Head Quarters who have been permitted to march with their divisions, and to report themselves to the Adjutant General's Office.

A. G. O.

ADJUTANT GENERAL's OFFICE.
Placencia, 9th July, 1809.

THE Commander of the Forces having arranged with the Magistrates of the different districts and towns in

Spain

Spain, that the Officers, Soldiers, and others belonging to the Army, are to be furnished with what they require, at the market prices, of each place where they may be quartered, makes known to the troops, that the Magistrates will cause to be put up, in the square or market place of each town or village, a List of the various articles of provisions, &c. &c. with their prices annexed to them ; and in case any of the inhabitants should demand a higher price than that fixed, the soldiers are to complain to their Officers, stating what inhabitants attempted to impose upon them, and the Commanding Officer of the regiment is to make known the soldier's complaint to the magistrates of the town, who will take proper measures on the occasion.

The soldiers are not, however, to attempt to take things by force, or on their own terms, under pretence that large prices have been demanded from them. Heads of Departments and persons attached to Head Quarters, in addition to putting up their names on the doors of their quarters, will always, on their arrival in a new quarter, immediately send their addresses to the Adjutant General, and to the Commandant at Head Quarters.

ADJUTANT GENERAL's OFFICE.
Placencia, 12th July, 1809.

GENERAL PASS ORDER,

THE General Court Martial, of which Major General M'Kenzie is President, is to assemble at Placencia to-morrow morning at ten o'clock.

ADJUTANT

ADJUTANT GENERAL'S OFFICE.

G. O. *Placencia, 13th July, 1809.*

ENSIGN D. Campbell, 3d Guards, is appointed Aide de Camp to Brigadier General H. Campbell from the 1st instant.

Mr. WEMYESS is appointed an Acting Assistant Commissary, until the pleasure of the Lords of the Treasury is known.

1. Such regiments as have Bakers who can bake biscuit, are immediately to send a list of their names to Mr. Deputy Commissary General Dalrymple, and to the Adjutant General's Office, and the bakers are to attend at the Deputy Commissary General's this evening, at 7 o'clock.

2. The attention of the General Officers is called to the orders of the 8th June, respecting the delivery of provisions by the Commissaries, and the Commander of the Forces begs to have from them a report that those orders have been complied with.

ADJUTANT GENERAL'S OFFICE.

G. O. *Placencia, 14th July, 1809.*

2. A BRIGADE of six-pounders is to be attached to each of the 1st, 2d, and 3d divisions of Infantry, and a brigade of three-pounders to the 4th division; the brigade of heavy six-pounders are to be in reserve.

3. The brigade of six-pounders ordered to be attached to the 3d division of Infantry need not join that division till further orders.

H 3

4. When

4. When a brigade of Artillery will be detached with a division of Infantry, the Officer commanding must give directions to the Commissary of one of the brigades of Infantry to provide the artillerymen, drivers, and horses, with provisions and forage.

5. The 1st Battalion 48th Regiment are to be in Brigadier General R. Stewart's brigade; the 1st battalion 61st in Brigadier General Anson's brigade; those Officers must see that those corps have copies of all the General Orders.

6. Robert Grierson, 29th regiment, is appointed to act as Purveyor's Clerk, and will report himself to Deputy Inspector Ferguson from the 13th instant.

7. In all future monthly returns, the total number of Non Commissioned Officers actually on service with the army, to be inserted on the face of the Return, in the column of drummers and serjeants present.

ADJUTANT GENERAL's OFFICE.

G. O. *Placencia, 15th July,* 1809.

1. IN consequence of the representations of the Lieutenant General commanding the cavalry, of the insufficiency of the allowance of the Veterinary Surgeons, and Farriers of the regiments of Dragoons, an additional allowance of three-pence for each horse per month to the former, and one half penny per day for each horse to the latter will be given; this allowance is to be drawn by the 3d Dragoon Guards, 4th Dragoons 16th, and 23d Light Dragoons, and 1st Light Dragoons King's German Legion, from the day each of these corps disembarked in Portugal, and by the 14th Light Dragoons from the 25th April.

2. *Extract*

2. Extract of a Letter from the Deputy Inspector of Hospitals to His Excellency the Commander of the Forces.

Many men have lately been sent to the Hospital, both here and elsewhere, in a state of the utmost filth, some with no shirts at all, and others with only one that had not been washed for any discoverable length of time; greater attention to cleanliness and the state of the men's necessaries seems therefore called for in some brigades of the army, and bathing whenever practicable, at an early hour in the morning, but at no other time ought to be universally practised during the hot season. The event species of contagious fever is infallibly generated among the troops by the neglect of personal cleanliness; new killed meat without salt is very prejudicial, and the mode of issuing and conducting the rations has been productive of much annoyance, exhaustion, and disappointment, and consequently of diseases to the soldiers.

3. The Commander of the Forces is concerned to state, that he has found those soldiers who were sent into hospitals in the shameful state reported by the Inspector of Hospitals, belonged to the 24th, 31st, and 45th regiments, and the German Light Dragoons; and he desires that more attention may be paid to the men's necessaries by the Officers in future.

4. It is very desirable that the Officers commanding companies should endeavour to procure salt in sufficient quantities for their men, and that the Officers commanding regiments should, if possible, make some arrangement for supplying the men with breakfast.

5. An advance of money will be issued this day to the regiments, on account of their estimates to the 24th July.

6. Captain

6. Captain Lord Burghurst, 3d Dragoon Guards, is appointed extra Aide-de-Camp to the Commander of the Forces.

7. The army will march on the 17th, and all the arrangements must be made in the course of this day and to-morrow, for leaving in the General Hospital such men as it will not be possible to move; subsistence to the 24th July must be left for such men as may be sent to General Hospitals, and Officers for the sick, in each brigade, according to the proportion in the General Orders 18th May. Commanding Officers of regiments will send this day to the Adjutant General, before 7 o'clock P. M., a return of carts attached to their regiments.

8. The Commissary General will this day make his arrangements with the Assistant Commissaries of brigades and regiments, to deliver to the troops at Placencia, to-morrow, four days bread, viz. 17th, 18th, 19th and 20th instant.

9. A General Court Martial will assemble to-morrow morning, at 11 o'clock, for the trial of such prisoners as may be brought before it.

Brigadier General A. Cameron, President.

	Field Officers.	Captains.	Subalterns.
Lieut. Gen. Sherbrook's Division .	2	1	2
Major Gen. Hill's do.	1	2	1
Brigadier Gen. Campbell's do. . .	0	1	1
Division of Cavalry	1	2	0
Total .	4	6	4

The

The name of the Officer appointed to act as Deputy Judge Advocate will be sent in the course of the day to the President, to whom a list of the Officers, with the dates of their commissions, will be sent.

G. O.

ADJUTANT GENERAL's OFFICE.
Placencia, 16th July, 1809.

AT a General Court Martial held at Placencia, 10th July, 1809, by order of his Excellency Lieutenant General Sir Arthur Wellesley, and of which Major General M'Kenzie was President, and Captain C. Collis, 24th Infantry, Deputy Judge Advocate, the Court being duly sworn proceeded to the trial of Lieutenant B. Dobbins, 66th Regiment, for sending a challenge to, and fighting a duel with, Lieutenant William Brodie, 66th Regiment, in which Lieutenant Brodie was killed, in the camp near Abrantes, 19th June, 1809; and the prisoner having pleaded not guilty, the Court proceeded to the examination of witnesses, and having maturely weighed the evidence produced in support of the charge, is of opinion the same is not proved, and does therefore acquit the prisoner, and he is hereby acquitted accordingly; which sentence has been confirmed by the Commander of the Forces.

The Court next proceeded to the trial of Captain Arthur Morris, 66th Regiment, for being second in a duel fought on the 19th June last, in the camp near Abrantes, between Lieutenants Brodie and Dobbins, 66th Regiment. The prisoner pleaded not guilty, and the Court

proceeded

proceeded to give public notice for the appearance of any person who could give evidence on the trial; but no person having appeared, in consequence of the said notice, the Court were of opinion the prisoner was not guilty of the crime laid to his charge, and do therefore acquit him; which sentence has been confirmed by his Excellency the Commander of the Forces.

The Court next proceeded to the trial of Lieutenant Henry Blake, 66th Regiment, tried for being second in a duel fought on the 19th June, 1809, in the camp near Abrantes, between Lieutenant Brodie and Lieutenant R. Dobbins, 66th Regiment; the prisoner pleaded not guilty. The Court then proceeded to give public notice for the appearance of any person who could give evidence on the trial; but no person appearing, in consequence of the said notice, the Court were of opinion that the prisoner was not guilty of the crime, and does therefore acquit him; which sentence was approved of by the Commander of the Forces.

The Court then proceeded to the trial of Private Henry Barnes, 6th Regiment, for refusing to march when ordered by Ensign Pepper, 87th Regiment, on or about the 12th May, 1809. The prisoner having pleaded not guilty, the Court proceeded to the examination of witnesses, and having maturely weighed the evidence produced in support of the prosecution, together with what the prisoner alleged in his defence, is of opinion that he is guilty of the crime laid to his charge, being a breach of the Articles of War, and do therefore sentence him to receive 600 Lashes, at such time and place as the Commander of the Forces shall think proper; which sentence has been approved of by the Commander of the Forces.

The

The Court next proceeded to the trial of John Dely, Private, 87th Regiment, for murder, committed on or about the 20th May, 1809, on the body of Private Owen Lahy, same regiment. The prisoner pleading not guilty, the Court proceeded to the examination of witnesses; the Court having deliberately weighed and considered the evidence in support of the charge, together with what the prisoner had said in his defence, is of opinion that he is guilty of the crime with which he is charged, being in breach of the Articles of War, and do therefore sentence him to suffer *Death* by being *hanged by the neck*, at such time and place as the Commander of the Forces may think proper; which sentence has been confirmed by his Excellency the Commander of the Forces.

The Court next proceeded to the trial of Patrick Mater, Private, 97th Regiment, for stealing a bundle of ball cartridges from the reserve ammunition under the charge of Mr. Conductor Tibbs, over which the prisoner was sentry, in the afternoon of the 11th July, 1809. The prisoner having pleaded not guilty, the Court proceeded to the examination of witnesses, and having maturely weighed the evidence, together with what the prisoner has said in his defence, is opinion he is guilty of the crime laid to his charge, being a breach of the Articles of War, and do therefore sentence him to receive 800 Lashes, at such time and place as the Commander of the Forces shall please to direct; which sentence has been confirmed by the Commander of the Forces.

1. The 40th and 97th Regiments, and 2d battalion detachments, and one company from each of the regiments of Infantry in camp, are to parade this evening on the ground of General Cameron's brigade, under the orders

orders of a General Officer, at 6 o'clock, in order to witness the execution of the sentences of the General Court Martial on the prisoners, Henry Barnes, 6th Regiment, John Dely, 87th Regiment, and Patrick Mater, 97th Regiment.

The Provost Marshal will attend to carry the sentences of the Court Martial into execution. The General Officer will receive his orders from the Adjutant General.

Brigadier General Anson for the above duty.

3. When the Commissary General is unable to issue wine to the troops, either on account of the scarcity of the article, or of the difficulty of issuing it, he must not interfere in any manner with the sale of wine where the troops may be quartered, or in the neighbourhood. The Provost Marshal and his Assistants will in that case take care that order is preserved in the wine-houses.

4. The Court Martial, of which Major General M'Kenzie was President, will re-assemble on the 18th instant, at the village of Miltados, at 12 o'clock.

5. Such Regimental Medical Officers as Mr. Deputy Inspector Furguson will require, must attend the sick in the hospitals at Placencia, till the Staff Surgeons will arrive.

ADJUTANT GENERAL's OFFICE.

A. G. O.   *Placencia, 16th July, 1809.*

MAJOR General Erskine being sick, Brigadier General Anson is appointed to command the brigade of Cavalry hitherto under the command of Major General Erskine, during his indisposition.

Th

The 61st Regiment is to be in General Cameron's brigade; the 40th Regiment in that hitherto under the command of Brigadier General Anson; Colonel Kemmis, of the 40th Regiment, is appointed a Colonel on the Staff till his Majesty's pleasure is known, and is to command the brigade of Infantry hitherto under the command of Brigadier General Anson.

G. A. O. ADJUTANT GENERAL's OFFICE.
Placencia, 16th July, 1809.

THE Assistant Adjutant General of the Division in which the brigade is that furnished the guards this day, will be responsible that they join their corps in the morning before they move off, except the ammunition guard at the Artillery Park, and the Provost guard, which remains as heretofore.

ADJUTANT GENERAL's OFFICE.
Placencia, 17th July, 1809.

MR. Melville is removed to General Cameron's brigade of Infantry, and will join them forthwith.

Mr. Myler will deliver charge of the stores, &c. in his possession to Mr. Melville, and proceed this day to join the 16th Light Dragoons.

Captain I. M. Cutcliffe, of the 23d Light Dragoons, is appointed Acting Deputy Assistant Quarter-Master General, till his Majesty's pleasure is known.

G. O.

Adjutant General's Office.
Orapesa, 20th July, 1809.

G. O.

THE Commander of the Forces wishes that the corps should be as strong as possible, and that no man should be left with baggage whom it is not absolutely necessary to leave in care of it.

The men's arms to be particularly examined this afternoon by the Officers; every man must have a good flint, and the dust must be well cleaned from the locks and touch-holes. The Commander of the Forces desires that the unmilitary practice of firing in the neighbourhood of the lines may be discontinued by the troops.

The Commissaries must give receipts or pay for whatever they may receive from the inhabitants of the country. The time of the Commander of the Forces yesterday was occupied in hearing complaints of the Commissaries having taken different articles of provisions without giving receipts for them, and he trusts that he will have no further ground for noticing this disobedience of orders.

HEAD-QUARTERS.
Orapesa, 21st *July,* 1809.

G. O.

THE army will march to-morrow morning; the regiments to be in the ranks as strong as possible.

The army will parade this evening, in marching order, at 5 o'clock, on the right of the high road from Orapesa towards Talavera de la Reyna, to be seen by General Cuesta;

Cuesta; the Infantry and Artillery formed in one line from the left, in the following order:

The 4th division with its left at the point near Orapesa, pointed out by the Commander of the Forces.

Major General Hill's division.

Lieutenant General Sherbrook's division.

Third division.

Lieutenant General Payne will receive directions from the Commander of the Forces where to form the Cavalry.

The troops will be at open ranks and will present arms, and Officers salute; drums and bands to play a march; each regiment, by word of command from its own Commanding Officer, when the General will approach its left.

The Commander of the Forces desires that mules, which will bring the provisions, may be allowed to go away as soon as the provisions will be delivered, and those who bring them will have got their receipts; the most serious inconvenience has already resulted from the detention of those mules.

G. O.   ADJUTANT GENERAL'S OFFICE.
Talavera de la Reyna, 22d July, 1809.

ONE third of each regiment to remain accoutred in their lines, and the whole must be on the alert.

Officers commanding regiments are to keep their Officers with their companies.

G. O.

ADJUTANT GENERAL's OFFICE.
Talavera de la Reyna, 25th July, 1809.

1. THE General Court Martial, of which General Cameron is President, is to re-assemble as soon as possible this day.

* * *

ADJUTANT GENERAL'S OFFICE.
Talavera de la Reyna, 26th July, 1809.

THE following Officers are appointed to the Staff of the army under the command of Lieutenant General Sir Arthur Wellesley:—Lieut. Richard D. Cane, 5th Dragoon Guards, to be Aide-de-Camp to Major General Lightburne; Captain Leonard Potter, 28th Foot, to be Brigade Major to Major General Lightburne; Ensign Chatham H. Churchill, 1st Foot Guards, to be Aide-de-Camp to Brigadier General C. Crawford; Captain Henry C. Dickens, 34th Foot, to be Brigade Major to Brigadier General C. Crawford.

* * *

PASS ORDER.

ADJUTANT GENERAL'S OFFICE.
Talavera de la Reyna, 27th July, 1809.

CAPTAIN the Honourable A. Gordon, of the 3d Foot Guards, Aide-de-Camp to the Commander in Chief, is appointed extra Aide-de-Camp to the Commander of the Forces.

ADJUTANT GENERAL'S OFFICE.

Talavera de la Reyna, 29th July, 1809.

G. O.

1. THE Commander of the Forces returns his thanks to the Officers and Troops, for their gallant conduct in the two trying days of yesterday and the day before, in which they have been engaged with, and beaten off the repeated attacks of, an army infinitely superior in number.

He has particularly to request that Lieutenant General Sherbrooke will accept his thanks, for the assistance he has received from him, as well as from the manner in which he led on the Infantry under his command to the charge of the bayonet. Major General Hill and Brigadier General Alexander Campbell are likewise entitled in a particular manner to the acknowledgments of the Commander of the Forces, for their gallantry and ability with which they maintained their posts against the attacks made upon them by the enemy.

The Commander of the Forces has likewise to acknowledge the ability with which the late Major General M'Kenzie (whose subsequent loss the Commander of the Forces laments) withdrew the division under his command from the out-posts, in front of the enemy's army, on the 27th instant; as well as to Colonel Donkin for his conduct on that occasion.

The Commander of the Forces likewise considers Lieutenant General Payne and the Cavalry, particularly Brigadier General Anson and his brigade, who was principally engaged with the enemy, to be entitled to his acknowledgments; as well as Brigadier General Howarth and his Artillery, Major General Tilson, Brigadier General R.

Stewart, Brigadier General Cameron, and the brigades under their commands, respectively.

He had opportunities of noticing the gallantry and discipline of the 5th battalion 60th, and the 45th, on the 27th, and of the 29th and 1st battalion 48th on that night, and on the 28th, of the 7th and 53d; and he requests their Commanding Officers, Major Davey, Colonel Guard, Colonel White, Colonel Donellan, Lieutenant Colonel Sir William Myers, and Lieutenant Colonel Bingham, to accept his particular thanks.

The charge made by the brigade of guards under the command of Brigadier General H. Campbell, on the enemy's attacking column, was a most gallant one; and the mode in which it was afterwards covered by the 1st battalion 48th, was most highly creditable to the most excellent corps, and to their Commanding Officer, Major Middlemore. The Commander of the Forces requests Colonel Fletcher, the Chief Engineer, Brigadier General the Honourable Charles Stewart, Adjutant General, Colonel Murray, Quarter-Master General, and the Officers of those departments respectively, and Lieutenant Colonel Bathurst and those of his personal Staff, will accept his thanks for the assistance he received from them throughout these trying days.

2. The bakers of the different brigades, who have already been employed by the Commissary General, will be sent immediately to his stores to receive his directions under a Non-commissioned Officer of Brigadier General Cameron's brigade, to parade at the Commander of the Forces, to receive instructions from Major Campbell, Assistant Adjutant General.

3. Two

3. Two camp kettles to be immediately sent from every regiment, for the wounded men in the General Hospital at Talavera.

4. Commanding Officers of regiments and brigades will direct that all arms, collected in the field of battle, may be sent in by a proper escort to such Artillery Stores as Brigadier General Haworth shall point out.

In the return of killed, wounded, and missing, directed to be sent in yesterday, attention must be paid to specify the same in two distinct returns, one of the 27th, and one of the 28th; as also to state the names of the Officers, killed, wounded, and missing, mentioning whether slightly or severely.

All prisoners and deserters to be sent to the Provost Marshal.

The names of the General and Staff Officers, killed, wounded, and missing, to be specified in the returns called for; these returns must be sent in to the Adjutant General's Office before 8 o'clock to-morrow morning at the latest.

G. PASS ORDER.

ADJUTANT GENERAL'S OFFICE.
Talavera de la Reyna, 29th July, 1809.

THE Commander of the Forces calls the attention of Officers commanding brigades and regiments, to prevent the practice of the soldiers firing off their muskets in camp; such men, whose arms cannot be drawn, must be regularly paraded, and their firelocks discharged at the same time.

I 2   G. A. O.

ADJUTANT GENERAL'S OFFICE.

G. A. O. *Talavera de la Reyna, 29th July,* 1809.

THE General Court Martial, of which Brigadier General Cameron was President, will assemble at Brigadier General Cameron's quarters at Talavera, at 12 o'clock to-morrow.

———————

ADJUTANT GENERAL'S OFFICE.

G. O. *Talavera de la Reyna, 30th July,* 1809.

2. THE Commissary General is to attend to the requisitions of the Inspector of Hospitals, for provisions and other articles for the sick and wounded. The brigades to appoint Officers and Non-commissioned Officers to take charge of the sick and wounded in general hospital, in proportion to their numbers, according to the General Orders.

3. These Officers and Non-commissioned Officers are to be selected from those who have slight wounds which are likely to detain them at Talavera, at the same time that they are not likely to be confined to their houses for any length of time.

A Field Officer to be appointed to superintend the military arrangements of the General Hospital; he will report to the Adjutant General what sentries will be necessary, and what guards will be required to furnish them.

The 1st division to furnish the Field Officer.

4. General Officers commanding brigades are desired to attend to the early and precise execution of all orders relating to the care of the sick and wounded, and to have

reports

reports made upon them according to the General Orders 4th July.

5. General Officers commanding divisions and brigades are desired this day to see that all the soldiers are supplied with ammunition and flints, &c. It is recommended to Officers commanding regiments to have the accoutrements of the killed and wounded men collected, which are laying about the ground. They will report to the Quarter-Master General the numbers collected, in order that arrangements may be made to procure store-houses for them at Talavera.

6. All persons having claims on the Paymaster General up to the 24th July, will receive payment of them the day after to-morrow, viz. Lieutenant General Sherbrook's, Major General Hill's, and the Cavalry, on that day. The 3d and 4th division and Head-Quarters on the following day.

The soldiers accounts are to be settled and closed to the 24th July, and their balances to be paid as soon as the Paymaster General shall have paid the balances due to the Regimental Paymasters on the estimates to the 24th July.

The Court Martial, of which the late Major General M'Kenzie was President, is dissolved.

G. PASS ORDER.

ADJUTANT GENERAL'S OFFICE.

Talavera de la Reyna, 30th July, 1809.

CAPTAIN Cockburne, 60th Regiment, Assistant Adjutant General, is appointed to do duty with the 4th divi-

sion,

sion, vice Cooke removed to Head-Quarters. Captain Cockburn will report himself to Brigadier General Campbell.

G. O.   *Talavera de la Reyna, 31st July,* 1809.

1. THE Commander of the Forces omitted, in his orders of the 29th instant, to draw the attention of the army to the conduct of the 97th Regiment, as reported by Brigadier General Campbell of the battalion 31st Regiment, on the 28th, as intended to have been reported by the late Major General M'Kenzie, and to that of the 1st battalion of detachments not having received these reports when the orders were issued. He begs that Lieutenant Colonel Lyon, Lieutenant Colonel Bunbury, and Major Watson, will accept his acknowledgments for the behaviour of the gallant corps under their command, respectively, and he will not fail to report their good conduct.

In the weekly states which became due to-morrow, an additional column of missing will be necessary.

Hospital Mate Moffat to do duty with the 2d battalion 48th as Assistant Surgeon.

G. O.   *Talavera de la Reyna, 1st Aug.* 1809.

1. THE 3d division is in future to be composed of Brigadier General R. Crawford's brigade of Infantry and Colonel Donkin's brigade, and will be under the command

mand of Brigadier General R. Crawford; Colonel Donkin's brigade is to consist of the 45th, 87th, 88th, and 5
companies 5th battalion 60th Regiment; 2d battalion 24th
are to be in General Cameron's brigade; 2d battalion 31st
in Brigadier General Tilson's.

3. Captain Taylor, 48th Regiment, is appointed Brigade Major to Brigadier General R. Stuart's brigade, vice
Gardner killed in action, from the 1st instant.

Brigade Major Balneave to be transferred from the
brigade of the late Major General M'Kenzie to that of
Brigadier General Cameron, vice Blair wounded.

4. Colonel Stopford is appointed a Colonel on the
Staff from the date hereof, and will command the brigade
of Guards during the indisposition, on account of his
wounds, of Brigadier General Campbell.

Captain Adams, Coldstream Guards, to act as Brigade
Major, vice Beckett killed in action.

6. Commissaries are to be posted to divisions, instead
of brigades of Infantry, in future, except to Lieutenant
General Sherbrook's, whose Commissaries will continue
attached as at present.

Mr. Dick to be Assistant Commissary to Major General Hill's division.

Mr. Fenlay, assisted by two Clerks, to the 3d division.

Mr. Wemyss, assisted by two Clerks, to the 4th division.

9. The General Court Martial, of which Brigadier
General Cameron is President, is dissolved.

10. At a General Court Martial held at Placencia in
June, and continued by adjournments, Private John Biggs,
40th Regiment, was tried for striking Ensign Pepper, of
the 87th Regiment, on or about the 7th May. The pri-

soner

soner pleading not guilty, the Court proceeded to the examination of witnesses, and having maturely weighed and considered the evidence of the prosecution, as well as what the prisoner has advanced in his defence, are of opinion that he is guilty of the crime laid to his charge, in breach of the Articles of War, and do therefore sentence him to receive 1000 Lashes, at such time and place as the Commander of the Forces shall think proper, which sentence has been confirmed by his Excellency.

11. Colonel Kemmis's brigade of Infantry and one company from each of the other brigades in camp to parade this evening, at 6 o'clock, in the lines, to see the sentence of the above Court Martial put in execution. The Provost Marshal will attend; Colonel Kemmis to call at the Adjutant General's Office for instructions.

ADJUTANT GENERAL'S OFFICE.

G. A. O.　　*Talavera de la Reyna, 1st Aug.* 1809.

IN consequence of the money not having arrived, the payments, as directed in the General Orders of the 29th July, will not be made until the 2d August, when they will take place in the following order, viz.—Lieutenant General Sherbrook's, Major General Hill's, and the Cavalry, on that day; the 3d and 4th divisions and head-quarters on the following day.

G. O.

<table>
<tr><td>G. O.</td><td>ADJUTANT GENERAL'S OFFICE.
Talavera de la Reyna, 2d Aug. 1809.</td></tr>
</table>

2. THE soldiers plunder the inhabitants bringing in provisions, notwithstanding the repeated orders given upon the subject, and the knowledge which they all have, that this practice must tend to their own distress.

3. The Commander of the Forces desires that particular attention may be paid to former orders, requiring that no soldier should quit his lines, excepting on fatigue, in charge of an Officer or Non-commissioned Officer, unless he is dressed according to the standing orders of his regiment with side-arms.

The rolls must be called in camp every two hours, and Commanding Officers of brigades will give directions what proportion of Officers of each regiment are to be present. The Provost and his Assistants must patrole the neighbourhood of the camp constantly, and the Assistants must relieve each other.

Serjeant-Major Pass, 2d battalion 28th Regiment, is appointed Assistant Provost Marshal to the battalion under the command of Brigadier General C. Crawford, from 25th ult.

The Rev. Samuel Briscall is appointed Chaplain to the Forces from 25th May.

G. AFTER

G. AFTER ORDERS.

ADJUTANT GENERAL'S OFFICE.
Talavera de la Reyna, 2d August, 1809.

SERJEANT Stanway, of the Coldstream Guards, is appointed an Assistant Provost Marshal to the army, and will remain at Talavera, reporting himself to Lieutenant Colonel M'Kinnon.

G. O.

ADJUTANT GENERAL'S OFFICE.
Meza de Iber, 6th August, 1809.

SUCH of the sick and wounded as are in the rear are to be victualled by the Commissaries attached to the divisions to which they happen to be nearest, and are to be brought on by them to-morrow to join the hospital at Delytosa.

Officers commanding divisions will see this order complied with.

Major Williamson is attached to the 2d division, vice Graham, who is attached to the third division until further orders.

The heavy brigade of six pounders to be attached to the 4th division, the Commissary of which is to provision it.

G. O.

ADJUTANT GENERAL'S OFFICE.
Delytosa, 9th August, 1809.

1. As the troops composing the army in Spain have not received their rations regularly since the 22d of July, it is not just that the full price of the ration should be

stopped

stopped from the soldier's pay; from the 23d July, therefore, the stoppage from the soldier's pay, on account of his rations, is to be only 3*d.* until the supplies are such as it will be possible to make regular deliveries of provisions. The Commander of the Forces will hereafter give notice of the period at which the full price of the rations is to be charged to the men: this order is applicable to the troops composing General Robert Crawford's brigade, only from the 30th July inclusive, and to the troops of Horse Artillery only from the 3d August.

2. The Commander of the Forces desires that the roll may be called in camp every two hours, and the Officers commanding divisions will give directions what proportion of Officers are to attend.

3. The soldiers themselves render the difficulties of the moment greater than they would otherwise be by their irregularity, as they seize and plunder the mules coming in with provisions, by which the good and regular soldiers of the army are deprived of their just share of them.

4. The Provost Marshal will ascertain by what roads provisions are coming in; he will take care that his Assistants patrole those roads constantly, and any man caught in the act of plundering provisions coming to the army, is to be punished on the spot as such a heinous offence deserves.

5. Soldiers must not quit their lines unless dressed with their side-arms, excepting when on fatigue; all soldiers on fatigue must be under the command of an Officer or Non-commissioned Officer.

6. The practice of taking roots and vegetables without paying for them must be entirely discontinued; if roots or vegetables are required, they must be taken by regular

parties

parties formed under the command of an Officer, who must take care and is responsible the owner of the ground is paid for what is taken.

7. When the sick and wounded under the charge of Colonel M'Kinnon move again, they will march in two divisions. The first will proceed under the medical care of Staff Surgeon Cooke, Mr. Rose, of the Guards, Mr. Thompson, 43d, Brooks, 87th, Mr. Juberger, 1st battalion King's German Legion, Mr. Thompson, 2d battalion King's German Legion, as his Assistants; this division will contain the most serious cases.

Second division will march under the medical care of Staff Surgeon Bell, Mr. Burke, 97th, Mr. Ward, 82d, Mr. Mosley, 45th, and Mr. Ireland, Rifle Corps King's German Legion, as his Assistants. The Commissary General will attach another Assistant Commissary to Colonel M'Kinnon, so that each division will be supplied with one. Acting Apothecary Trigou will accompany the first division with his stores. 24th, 45th, 1st and 2d battalions 48th, will send each a Serjeant in the course of the day to assist in taking charge of their wounded at the Convent; they are to remain with the sick until further orders.

8. A small supply of shoes and camp kettles being ready for delivery at Delytosa, regiments will send in returns of these articles wanting immediately to the Quarter-Master General, as the issues must be made in the course of the day.

9. A General Court Martial will assemble to-morrow at 10 o'clock, at Delytosa, for the trial of such prisoners as may be brought before it.

Brigadier

Brigadier General Richard Stewart, President.

	Field Officers.	Captains.	Subalterns.
1st Division - - - - - - - - - - - - - - -	3 —	2 —	1
2d ditto - - - - - - - - - - - - - - -	1 —	2 —	1
4th ditto - - - - - - - - - - - - - - -	1 —	2 —	1
Total - - - -	5 —	6 —	3

G. PASS ORDER.

Adjutant General's Office.
Deleytosa, 9th August, 1809.

The General Court Martial, of which Brigadier General R. Stewart is President, ordered to assemble to-morrow, is deferred until further orders.

G. O.

Adjutant General's Office.
Deleytosa, 10th August, 1809.

1. The Paymaster General will this day make an advance to the Paymasters of the different corps equal to one-half of their subsistence, from the 25th July to the 24th August, calculating the subsistence at 6*d.* per diem.

G. O.

ADJUTANT GENERAL's OFFICE.

G. O.   *Jaracejo, 11th August,* 1809.

THE Army are desired to attend particularly to the orders relative to the watering their horses, until two hours before or after feeding.

ADJUTANT GENERAL's OFFICE.

A. G. O.   *Jaracejo, 12th August,* 1809.

LIEUTENANT Garland, of the 1st battalion of detachments, having in a most disgraceful manner quitted the army without leave, when engaged in operations against the enemy, is to be put in arrest by the Commanding Officer of the 1st British detachment or garrison he will approach, and is to be sent to the army without loss of time.

Commanding Officers of Regiments are to report immediately to the Adjutant General the names of all Officers who have absented themselves, without leave, since the 25th of last month, in order that their names may be published in the Orders of the Army, and that they may be ordered to the army in arrest.

ADJUTANT GENERAL's OFFICE.

G. O.   *Jaracejo, 13th Aug.* 1809.

1. REGIMENTAL Surgeons are desired to transmit the usual weekly and monthly reports of sick, to the Inspector of Hospitals' Head Quarters.

2. As

2. As there is no General Hospital establishment, Regimental Surgeons will take charge of their own sick.

3. Regimental Surgeons are directed to purchase any medicines which they may absolutely require; the Paymaster of the regiment, under the authority of the Commanding Officer, will advance money to defray the expence, agreeable to His Majesty's Regulations for the guidance of Regimental Surgeons, dated 1808.

The charge for medicines will be included in their contingent accounts, and upon producing the proper vouchers will be approved of by the Inspector of Hospitals.

Doctor Franks, Inspector of Hospitals, having arrived at the army, is to have the chief superintendence of the Medical Department.

ADJUTANT GENERAL'S OFFICE.

G. PASS ORDER.　*Juracejo, 14th August,* 1809.

A COURT of Inquiry to assemble immediately at the camp, to investigate such matters as will be laid before it. The Court will assemble at the tent or hut of the President.

1st Division gives the Field Officer President.

	Captains.		Subalterns.
1st Division	1	—	2
2d do.	2	—	1
4th do.	1	—	1
Total	4	—	4

G. O.

ADJUTANT GENERAL's OFFICE.

G. O.   *Jaracejo, 15th August, 1809.*

1. THE General Court Martial, of which Brigadier General R. Stewart is President, directed to assemble by the General Orders of the 9th instant, will meet to-morrow morning, at 9 o'clock, at the Adjutant General's Office; all evidences to attend, names and dates of Commissions of the members to be sent to the Adjutant General's Office immediately.

2. The detail for the General Court Martial will be as follows, instead of that specified in the General Orders of the 9th.

Brigadier General R. Stewart, President.

	Field Officers.	Captains.
1st Division	3 —	3
2d do.	1 —	3
4th do.	1 —	3
Total . .	5	9

ADJUTANT GENERAL's OFFICE.

G. O.   *Jaracejo, 16th August, 1809.*

1. THE Soldiers are again positively prohibited to plunder bee-hives; any man found with a bee-hive in his possession will be punished.

2. The rolls to be called in camp every two hours: the Officers commanding divisions will settle what number of Officers of each regiment are to attend.

3. The

3. The Provost must patrole in the neighbourhood of the camp, and every man found out of his lines without his accoutrements, and not dressed as a soldier ought to be, is to be punished.

Men sent on fatigue will be under the command of an Officer, or Non-Commissioned Officer.

4. The Commissary General to send immediately to the Adjutant General's Office, a return of the number of men employed by him as Guards, specifying whether upon cattle, or stores, in order that an arrangement may be made for their regular relief.

════════════

ADJUTANT GENERAL'S OFFICE.

G. O. *Truxillo, 20th August,* 1809.

AT a General Court Martial held at Jaracejo, by order of His Excellency Lieutenant General Sir Arthur Welles-ley, and of which Brigadier General R. Stewart was President, and Captain Goodman, of the 48th regiment, Acting Deputy Judge Advocate, Lieutenant David Beatty, of the 53d regiment, was arraigned on the following charges, viz.

1st, For absenting himself from his Quarter Guard, the whole or greater part of the night of the 5th August, being a breach of the Articles of War, and contrary to good order and military discipline.

2d, For quitting his Platoon, or Division, during the march on the 8th of August, and refusing or neglecting to join it, when repeatedly ordered by Major Thirsby, of the said regiment, being contrary to good order and military discipline.

3d, For absenting himself from the whole or greater part of the march, on the morning of the 10th instant, being in breach of the Articles of War, and contrary to good order and military discipline.

To which charges, the prisoner Lieutenant David Beatty, pleaded not guilty. The Court proceeded to the examination of witnesses, and having maturely weighed and considered the evidence adduced on the prosecution in support of the charges against the prisoner Lieutenant David Beatty, 53d regiment, together with what he offered in his defence, are of opinion that he is guilty of the charges preferred against him (with the exception of the latter part of the 2d charge, viz. for refusing or neglecting to join his platoon or division when ordered by Major Thirsby, of the said regiment,) being a breach of the Articles of War, and do therefore sentence the prisoner Lieutenant David Beatty, of the 53d regiment, to be suspended from rank and pay for the space of six calender months, from the 16th August; which sentence has been confirmed by His Excellency the Commander of the Forces.

2. The Adjutant of the Fusileers being wounded and a prisoner, Serjeant Major Hay, of the 53d regiment, is appointed to act as Adjutant to the Fusileers.

3. The Commissaries of the 1st Division will furnish the sick of Major General Hill's division with provisions, until they join their divisions.

4. Officers commanding corps will give particular directions that the men having charge of cars, are not to load them above 600lb. weight, the utmost they can carry ; the consequence must be, if this order is not complied with, that cars must break down, and cannot now be replaced.

5. The

5. The troops will march to-morrow by orders they will receive from the Quarter-Master General. The sick will proceed, as this day, under the charge of Captain Cemetiere, 48th regiment, from whom all Officers in charge of sick will receive directions.

6. A ration of spirits will be issued to the troops at Truxillo this day: Commanding Officers of corps will immediately send parties on fatigue to the Commissary General's to receive the same.

ADJUTANT GENERAL'S OFFICE.

G. O.　　　　　*Truxillo, 21st August,* 1809.

1. THE following Officers of the Army have absented themselves since the 25th July, 1809.

Rank and Names.	Regiments.	Since what Time.	Remarks.
As. Surg. Hickson	4 Dragoons	5 Aug. 1809.	
Lieut. Spooner	23 Dragoons	. . . .	Left sick at Talavera, and had charge of a detachment of the regt. which remained until the day after the army marched; Lieutenant Spooner has not been heard of since.
Paym. I. Buxton	2 Bn. 24 Regt.		
Paym. Tho. Stott	29th Regt.	. . . .	Missing on the regiment leaving Talavera; supposed to be taken by the enemy.
Ens. T. O. Reeves	2 Bn. 48 Regt.	27 July, 1809	Absented himself soon after the commencement of the firing, and has never been since seen
Lt. W. Garland	{ 91st Regt. / 1 Bn. Detac. }	3 Aug. 1809.	

Paym.

Paym. M. Dalhunty 45th Regt. . . . . {Had leave to go from camp to Talavera on the morning of the march, in charge of a considerable sum of money received the night before from the Paymaster General, since which time he has not been heard of.

Paym. A. Thompson 53d Regt. 1 Aug. 1809.

2. The following General and Staff Officers names should have appeared in the orders of the 26th July last.

Major General S. Lightburne.

Brigadier General R. Crawford.

Brigadier General C. Crawford.

Captain Wm. Campbell, 7th Light Dragoons, to be Aide-de-Camp to Brigadier General R. Crawford.

Captain Charles Rowan, 52d regiment, to be Brigade Major to Brigadier General R. Crawford.

G. A. O.

ADJUTANT GENERAL'S OFFICE.
Truxillo, 21st August, 1809.

THE Commander of the Forces has been pleased to direct, that Mr. Assistant Commissary Gordon be dismissed from his situation as Assistant Commissary, in consequence of the representations of Mr. Deputy Commissary General Dalrymple, and Mr. Irwine, Surgeon to the Forces.

Mr. Richardson, of the Commissariat department, is appointed to act as Assistant Commissary to the 4th Dragoons until further orders.

G. O.

Adjutant General's Office.

G. O.   *Medellen, 23d August,* 1809.

. 1. Officers commanding divisions and brigades will be pleased to take measures to prevent the women, and followers of the army, buying up the bread which is prepared for the soldiers' rations : this practice, carried on in the irregular manner as it is at present, must ultimately prejudice the soldiers, and prevent the regular supply of bread.

2. Captain Cimitire, 48th regiment, in charge of the sick, having reported himself unwell, he will be relieved by a Captain of the 4th division ; and as the sick increase from the number of men that are straggling in from the divisions, a Field Officer, from the 1st division, will superintend and have charge of them in future: he will immediately wait on the Adjutant General for instructions. The Provost Marshal will attach an Assistant to march with the sick.

3. Paymaster Stott, 29th regiment, is to be put under an arrest, by the Officer commanding that corps, for absenting himself from the army at Talavera.

Adjutant General's Office.

G. PASS ORDER.   *Medillen, 23d August,* 1809.

The women of the army must be prevented from purchasing bread in the villages within two leagues of the station of any division of the army ; when any woman wants to purchase bread, she must ask the Officer of the Company to which she belongs for a pass-port, which must be countersigned by the Commanding Officer of the regiment; any woman found with bread in her possession, purchased

      at

at any place nearer than two leagues, will be deprived of the bread by the Provost, or his Assistants; as will any woman who goes out of camp to purchase bread without a passport.

Women who will have been discovered disobeying this order, will not be allowed to receive rations.

ADJUTANT GENERAL'S OFFICE.

G. A. O.   *Medillen, 23d August,* 1809.

THE four battalions of the King's German Legion are to be considered as one Brigade, under the command of Brigadier General Low, until further orders.

ADJUTANT GENERAL'S OFFICE.

G. O.   *Merida, 24th August,* 1809.

1. THE Paymasters of regiments, and all persons having claims on the Paymaster General, are to receive the balances due to them to the 24th August, to-morrow: this includes Staff Officers.

2. The stoppage from the pay of Non-Commissioned Officers and soldiers on account of rations, is to be only 3d. per diem. Soldiers accounts are to be settled forthwith, and they are to receive their balances accordingly.

3. Paymaster Dalhunty, 45th regiment, Paymaster Buxton, 24th regiment, and Paymaster Knight, of the King's German Legion, who joined the army this day, having absented themselves from the army at Talavera without leave, are to be placed under arrest by their respective Commanding Officers.

G. O.

ADJUTANT GENERAL'S OFFICE.

G. O. Merida, 25th August, 1809.

Memorandum.—In the monthly Returns due on this day, the column of recruiting is to be altered to that of missing in the rank and file; the serjeants and drummers missing are to be included in the column of Non-Commissioned Officers present, and stating the number of each rank missing at the bottom; when casualties occur amongst the serjeants and drummers, they are to be included in the respective columns in the alterations since last return, but it is, notwithstanding, to be noticed at the bottom of the return that such casualties are included.

The casualties amongst Officers to be inserted at the bottom, and their names specified.

1. Lieutenant Lord James Hay is appointed Aide-de-Camp to Lieutenant General Sherbrooke.

2. Lieutenant W. R. Hoey, 18th Hussars, having joined the army from England, is attached to the Adjutant General's department.

3. The army must not take forage for themselves, but must get it from the Commissary according to the usual mode, by sending in returns of the number of animals for whom forage is required, and receiving from him the regular rations; or if forage cannot be provided in that mode, and it is necessary it should be taken from the fields, it must be taken according to the General Orders of the 17th of June, 1809.

4. The Court Martial of which Brigadier General R. Stewart is President, will assemble to-morrow morning, at 10 o'clock, at the Adjutant General's Office.

K 4

G. O.

ADJUTANT GENERAL'S OFFICE.

G. O.　　　　　*Merida, 26th August,* 1809.

1. PAYMASTER A. Thompson, 53d regiment, is to be placed under an arrest by the Officer commanding that corps, for absenting himself at, or near Talavera, and proceeding to the rear to Elvas without leave.

ADJUTANT GENERAL'S OFFICE.

G. A. O.　　　　　*Merida, 26th August,* 1809.

A GENERAL Court Martial will assemble at Niza, for the trial of such prisoners as may be brought before it.

Brigad.er General C. Crawford, President.

Captain Cockburn, 60th regiment, Acting Deputy Assistant Adjutant General, Acting Deputy Judge Advocate.

The detail for the Court Martial to be furnished by the Deputy Assistant Adjutant General attached to Brigadier General C. Crawford's corps.

ADJUTANT GENERAL'S OFFICE.

G. A. O.　　　　　*Merida, 26th July,* 1809.

The General Court Martial, of which Brigadier General R. Stewart is President, to assemble to-morrow morning at 9 o'clock, and all evidences to attend.

G. O,

Adjutant General's Office.

Merida, 27th August, 1809.

G. O.

1. At a General Court Martial held at Jaracejo, and continued by adjournments, of which Brigadier General R. Stewart was President, and Captain Goodman, 48th Regiment, Deputy Judge Advocate, the Court proceeded to the trial of John Wilkinson, Conductor of Stores, arraigned on the following charge, viz. For absenting himself from his duty, on or about the 27th July, when in the evening of that day, and during the action, he quitted his situation, having charge of spare ammunition, taking a horse, a Gunner Driver, and another horse with him, making the best of his way to Placencia, and spreading infamous reports on the road injurious to the British army, saying it had been defeated by the enemy, and propagating many other things to the prejudice of good order and military discipline, to which charge the prisoner pleaded not guilty. The Court proceeded to the examination of witnesses, and having maturely and deliberately weighed and considered the evidence against the prisoner, John Wilkinson, Conductor of Stores, together with what he urged in his defence, are of opinion he is guilty of the charge preferred against him, being in breach of the Articles of War, and do sentence him, the prisoner, John Wilkinson, Conductor of Stores, to be dismissed his Majesty's service, and rendered incapable of serving his Majesty in any military capacity whatever; which sentence has been confirmed by the Commander of the Forces.

2. The Court then proceeded to the trial of Captain C.

Patrickson,

Patrickson, 43d Regiment, arraigned on the following charge, viz. Neglect of duty, on or about the 13th July, 1809; to which charge the prisoner pleaded not guilty, and the Court proceeded to the examination of witnesses; and the Court having maturely weighed and considered the evidence adduced on the prosecution in support of the charge against the prisoner, together with what he has alleged in his defence, and the evidence thereon, are of opinion he is not guilty of the charge preferred against him, and do therefore fully acquit him of the same; which sentence has been confirmed by his Excellency the Commander of the Forces.

3. Captain Patrickson is to be immediately released from his arrest.

4. The Commander of the Forces begs to call the attention of the Officers of the army to the orders of the 29th May, 1809. General Officers commanding divisions and brigades are requested to have the orderly books of those regiments examined which arrived in Portugal since the 1st of May last, and they will have inserted in them, and read to the soldiers, all orders of regulations, if any there be, which have not been issued to them.

5. John Wilkinson is to continue under charge of the Provost until an opportunity shall offer of sending him to Lisbon; he is to receive his rations only.

6. Paymasters of regiments are to give in two supplementary estimates for the difference between 6*d.* and 3*d.* stoppages per day from each man's pay, for his rations; the first for the 23d and 24th July; the other from the 25th July to the 24th August.

Paymasters of regiments, in Brigadier General R. Crawford's

Crawford's brigade, are to give in one supplementary estimate, from the 30th July to 24th August, for the same difference.

7. The troops having again received their full rations, and the Commander of the Forces having reason to believe, they will receive them regularly, the regiments in the 1st, 2d, and 4th divisions of Infantry, the Artillery, and General Fane's brigade of Cavalry, are to be under the usual stoppages of 6*d*. per diem for rations, from the 25th instant inclusive: as soon as reports are received from the 3d division and General Cotton and Anson's brigades of Cavalry, orders will be given to fix the period at which the stoppage of 6*d*. per day is to commence with them.

8. Commanding Officers of regiments are referred to the General Orders, (No. 3. of the 31st May,) requiring them to send in returns of bill-hooks, camp kettles, &c.

9. As shirts and shoes for the army are on the road from Lisbon, Commanding Officers of regiments are requested, as soon as possible, to send in returns to the Quarter-Master General of the number of shirts and pairs of shoes they will require to complete each man with two good shirts and two good pairs of shoes.

10. Surgeon Rob, 95th Regiment, to be Surgeon to the Forces. Assistant Surgeon Bourke, 97th Regiment, to be Surgeon to the 95th Regiment.

11. The Commander of the Forces has been pleased to grant all the Assistant Provosts of the army bât and forage allowance of Ensigns.

Mr. James Dick, 52d Regiment, has the Commander of the Forces leave to remain in the Commissariat Department till further orders.

G. O.

ADJUTANT GENERAL'S OFFICE.
Merida, 28th August, 1809.

G. O.

1. PAYMASTER Knight, 5th Line battalion King's German Legion, is released from his arrest, his Commanding Officer having certified that extreme indisposition was the cause of his having absented himself from the army at Talavera.

2. Paymaster Thomas Stott, 29th Regiment, is released from his arrest, the Commanding Officer of the corps, Lieutenant Colonel White, having certified that extreme sickness was the cause of his having absented himself from the army at Talavera.

ADJUTANT GENERAL'S OFFICE.
Merida, 29th August, 1809.

G. O.

1. THE General Court Martial, of which Brigadier General R. Stewart is President, re-assembled at Merida on the 27th instant, proceeded to the trial of John Davis, Private, 40th Regiment, arraigned on suspicion of robbing the military chest. The prisoner pleaded not guilty, and the Court proceeded to the examination of witnesses, and having maturely and deliberately considered the evidence against the prisoner, John Davis, together with what he offers in his defence, are of opinion there is not sufficient evidence to substantiate the charge preferred against the prisoner, John Davis, and do acquit him thereof; which sentence has been confirmed by his Excellency the Commander of the Forces. Private John

Davis

Davis is to be immediately released and sent to his regiment.

2. The Court next proceeded to the trial of Serjeant John Matthews, 2d battalion 48th Regiment, arraigned for irregular and unsoldier-like conduct, by prevaricating grossly in giving his testimony before the General Court Martial, of which Brigadier General Richard Stewart was President, on the 27th of August. The prisoner pleaded not guilty, and the Court proceeded to the examination of witnesses, and having considered the evidence against the prisoner and what he offers in his defence, are of opinion he is guilty of the charge preferred against him, being a breach of the Articles of War, and do sentence him to be reduced to the rank and pay of a private; which sentence has been confirmed by his Excellency the Commander of the Forces.

3. The General Court Martial, of which Brigadier General Richard Stewart is President, is dissolved.

G. PASS ORDER.

ADJUTANT GENERAL'S OFFICE.
Merida, 29th August, 1809.

A BOARD, of a Field Officer and two Captains from the 1st division, to assemble immediately at the Commissary General's to examine and report upon some calico and checked shirts received for the army.

To state particularly, if serviceable, what their value may be, comparing them with the shirts the men are generally furnished with.

G. PASS

G. PASS ORDER.

ADJUTANT GENERAL'S OFFICE.
Merida, 29th August, 1809.

SURGEONS of regiments will apply to the Commissary General to receive an issue of wine for such of their sick as require it.

G. O.

ADJUTANT GENERAL'S OFFICE.
Merida, 30th August, 1809.

1. CAPTAIN S. A. Goodman, 1st battalion 48th regiment, is appointed Deputy Judge Advocate to the army from the 25th instant.

2. A General Court Martial will assemble to-morrow morning, at 10 o'clock, at the Adjutant General's Office.

Major General Tilson, President.

	Field Officers.	Captains.	Subalterns.
1st Division	2 —	4 —	2
2d ditto	2 —	3 —	1
Total . .	4 —	7 —	3

A list of the Officers and dates of their commissions will be sent in the course of this day, directed to Captain Goodman, Deputy Judge Advocate, at the Adjutant General's Office.

G. O.

ADJUTANT GENERAL'S OFFICE.
Merida, 1st Sept. 1809.

G. O.

THE following Regulations, respecting the issue of bât and forage money having been approved of by his Majesty, are to be conformed to accordingly.

Allowances of Forage Money to the General and Staff Officers serving on Foreign Stations.

	No. of Rations per Day, at 6d. each.
General or Officer commanding the Forces . .	100
Lieutenant General	60
Major General	40
Brigadier General	30
Adjutant General	20
Deputy Adjutant General	15
Assistant Adjutant General	10
Deputy Assistant Adjutant General	6
Quarter-Master General	20
Deputy Quarter-Master General	15
Assistant Quarter-Master General	10
Deputy Assistant Quarter-Master General . .	6
Military Secretary	10
Aide-de-Camp	10
Brigade Major	10
Surgeon to the General commanding	10
Provost Marshal	3
Deputy Provost Marshal	3
Baggage Master General	10

Bridge

Bridge Master 10
Captain of Guides 10
Deputy Judge Advocate 10
Commissary of Accounts 20
Deputy Commissary of Accounts 15
Assistant Commissary of Accounts 10
Commissary of Provisions 15
Deputy Commissary of Provisions 6
Commissary General 40
Deputy Commissary General 15
Assistant Commissaries, (each) 10
Inspecting Commissary 10
Inspector of Hospitals 30
Deputy Inspector of Hospitals 15
Physicians 12
Purveyor 14
Deputy Purveyor 6
Surgeon 8
Apothecary 6
Hospital Mate 2
Brigade Chaplain 10
Inspector of Foreign Corps 10
Town or Fort Major 10
Town or Fort Adjutant 3

Colonel

	Rations of Forage Money, at 6d. per Day.	Baggage Money.	Bât Money.
		£. s. d.	£. s. d
Colonel commanding a battalion	11	7 10 0	10 0 0
Colonel commanding	9	7 10 0	10 0 0
Lieut. Colonel commanding . .	10	7 10 0	0 0 0
Lieut. Colonel not commanding	8	7 10 0	10 0 0
Major commanding	9	7 10 0	10 0 0
Major not commanding	7	7 10 0	10 0 0
Captain commanding	7	7 10 0	10 0 0
Captain with company.	5	7 10 0	10 0 0
*Company Captain absent . . .	2	————	10 0 0
Subalterns, (each)	1	3 15 0	————
Adjutant	1	5 0 0	————
Quarter-Masters of Cavalry . .	1	————	————
Quarter-Masters of Infantry . .	1	5 0 0	————
Surgeon	5	7 10 0	10 0 0
Assistant Surgeon	1	3 15 0	————
Paymaster	5	7 10 0	10 0 0
*Captain without company . . .	3	7 10 0	————

Regulations relative to Bât and Forage Money.

1. The period at which 200 days bât, baggage, and forage money is issued, must depend on local circumstances, to be determined by the General commanding in each particular service; but when 165 days forage money in the same year is ordered to be issued, it is to be understood that neither bât nor baggage money is included.

2. Deputies acting in the absence of their principals to receive the same as if they were at the head of the Department, provided their principals have not or do not receive it. Assistants succeeding to the charge of Staff Departments to receive the same as Deputies.

3. Regimental Officers having Brevet rank, to receive the proportion allotted to that rank, and not according to their regimental commissions.

4. An Officer holding two commissions, or two employments, of any kind, to receive for one only.

5. To enable them to equip themselves for field service, all Officers (Staff or Regimental) ordered for the first time to join an army on foreign service, if they embark during the period on which 200 days bât, baggage, and forage money was issued to the troops on that service, to be permitted to receive that allowance, whatever the period of their arrival may be; in like manner, if they embark during the period of the issue of 165 days forage money, to be permitted to receive that allowance, unless, however, they shall have received at any time, previous to their embarking, or are to receive, any outfit money or sums, by any other name or denomination, on the above account, in which case such sums are to be deducted; but Officers (either Staff or Regimental) being absent on leave on account of ill health or private affairs, on their returning to their duty are not to receive bât, baggage, and forage money, unless they shall produce proper certificates that they have embarked not later than 61 days after the period when such allowance commences, and it shall appear to the Officer commanding, that they have used due diligence in repairing to their duty.

6. In bât and forage allowance given to each company, the bât money and two rations of forage being allowed for the service of the company, the Officer actually commanding the company is to receive it in the first instance, and any Officer taking the command during the period of the issue, is entitled to receive from him a due proportion of that money for the remainder of the period: this regulation also applies to the bât money and two rations of forage issued to the Paymaster and Surgeon.

7. Officers

7. Officers who may obtain promotion or be appointed to Staff situations, provided it is notified in orders to the army to which they belong before half the period for which bât and forage money has been issued expires, to be entitled to receive the difference between the sums paid to them in their former rank and the rank or situation to which they are promoted or appointed; Staff situations are not to receive any difference of bât or forage money, if their promotions or appointments are notified subsequent to half the period for which bât and forage money has been issued.

Supplementary returns, according to the following form, are to be immediately sent in to the Quarter-Master General for all claims to additional allowances for the last 200 days issue arising from the above regulations.

Supplementary Returns of Officers of the Regiment of for 200 Days Bât, Baggage, and Forage Money.

Rank and Names.	No. of Rations at 6d.	Forage Money.	Baggage Money.	Bât Money.	Total.	Remarks.
		£. s. d.	£. s. d.	£. s. d.	£. s. d.	

The period of the late issue of 200 days bât and forage allowance is considered as having commenced on the 1st of March, and as ending on the 16th of September.

Officers

Officers having claims under regulations *No. 5*, must state the date of their embarkation and that of their arrival with the army, as also whether they have previously received any of the other allowances therein mentioned, and whether returning to their duty or joining for the first time.

Officers having claims under the regulations *No. 7*, must state the date of their promotion or appointment.

ADJUTANT GENERAL's OFFICE.
Badajoz, 3d Sept. 1809.

G. O.

As the Commander of the Forces proposes that the troops shall remain in the stations in which they are now or will shortly be placed as long as circumstances will permit, he desires that the Officers commanding regiments will send to Lisbon, as soon as possible, an Officer belonging to the regiment under their command respectively, in order to get from the regimental stores such articles of clothing, accoutrements, and necessaries as the soldiers require.

The names of the Officers sent upon this duty are to be sent in to the Quarter-Master General; these Officers on their arrival at Lisbon are to report themselves to the Assistant Quarter-Master General stationed there, and are to give him a list of the articles which they will have been directed to send up to their regiments, specifying the weight of the whole, and, as far as possible, of each article. They will likewise report to him the day on which the articles required will be ready to quit Lisbon, and they will obey such directions as they will receive from

this

this Officer respecting the transport of the baggage, whether by land or by water.

The Assistant Quarter-Master General at Lisbon having received from the Officers before mentioned, the returns of the baggage required for their regiments and the weight, will make requisitions upon the Commissary for boats, and carts to transport it to the army, taking care to allow no more to be put on each cart, drawn by two bullocks, than 600 pounds weight. The Officer in command of the troops at Lisbon will give such assistance of fatigue parties to the Officer's going down for baggage as they may have occasion for.

Such sick men as cannot march must be sent to the hospital at Elvas.

Colonel M'Kinnon will order from the hospital at Elvas to join their corps, such Officers and Soldiers as are fit to do their duty, keeping at Elvas only the proportion of Officers and Non-commissioned Officers for the number of each brigade in the hospital, according to the General Order of the 18th May.

The 83d, and 87th regiments, and the two battalions of detachments, need not send to Lisbon for their baggage.

ADJUTANT GENERAL's OFFICE.
Badajoz, 14th Sept. 1809.

G. O.

1. THE 11th regiment are to join and form part of Brigadier General A. Campbell's brigade ; the 2d battalion, 42d regiment, to join and form part of Brigadier General Cameron's brigade ; the 57th regiment to join and form part of Brigadier General Richard Stewart's brigade.

L 3

The

The 2d battalion 28th, 2d battalion 34th, and 2d battalion 39th, to be a brigade under the command of Brigadier General Catlin Crawford, which brigade is, till further orders, to be in the 2d division of the army under the command of Major General Hill.

2. Paymasters of regiments are, as soon as possible, to send their estimates of subsistence from the 25th August, to the 24th September, upon the amount of which, the Paymaster General will make to each an advance of one third.

3. Whenever a soldier is sent to the General Hospital, subsistence at the rate of 9d. per diem is to be sent with him, to the end of the muster.

4. The Commander of the Forces requests the attention of the General Officers commanding divisions and brigades to the General Orders of the 4th July, respecting the early obedience to orders.

5. The Commissary General is to make immediate arrangements for the payment in ready money, by the Assistant Commissaries attached to divisions, brigades, &c. for supplies they will receive, and for this purpose he will this day send off, to each of them, sufficient sums of money; and he will take care, and is held responsible, that they are hereafter fully and regularly supplied with money.

6. The General Officers commanding divisions and brigades, are requested to report to the Commander of the Forces, if the Assistant Commissaries should neglect to obey these orders.

7. The hospital at Abrantes is to be removed to Lisbon, the Officers and soldiers able to do their duty must be sent to join the army. Of the sick and convalescents, the men unable to march must be sent down in boats, halting

each

each night at the place pointed out in the route for those who will march. The Quarter-Master General, and the Commanding Officer, and the Commissary at Abrantes, will take measures for carrying this order into execution.

8. The Commanding Officer at Lisbon is to send to join the army, without loss of time, every Officer in the medical department, not absolutely required for the attendance on the hospital at Lisbon; the Commanding Officer at Lisbon will, once a week, compare the state of the Hospital Staff at Lisbon, with the number of sick men in the hospital, and will order to the army such Medical Officers as he may think not required to attend to the number of sick in the hospital. All Medical Officers arriving from England are to be sent to join the army without loss of time. The General Officer at Lisbon will order to join their regiments, all Officers and soldiers who are sufficiently well to do their duty.

9. The Commander of the Forces desires that the following orders may be added to those already given out for the regulation of the hospital of the army.

10. The soldiers in the hospitals must not be allowed to straggle about the towns in which the hospitals are stationed, and all men found at the distance of one street from the hospital, must be tried and punished for the disobedience of orders. The rolls of the hospital must be called once every hour, in the presence of an Officer, or such number of Officers as the Commanding Officer at the hospital will appoint to attend to the roll calling.

11. All men absent from roll calling, to be tried and punished for disobedience of orders.

12. The soldiers in hospital, or convalescent at the station where the hospital is, and victualled by the Commis-

sary,

sary, or on the route to join their regiments, are not to receive wine unless directions in writing should be given by the Medical Officer, that they are to receive it; and the Medical Officer is particularly desired not to give those directions unless in cases in which it may have appeared to him that the soldiers have conducted themselves as they ought in the hospital, and in such a manner as to secure their early recovery.

13. As comforts for the sick can now be got, the regimental hospitals are to be established upon the plan ordered by His Majesty's regulations, and the soldiers are to be under the usual stoppage while in hospital.

G. A. O.
ADJUTANT GENERAL'S OFFICE.
Badajoz, 4th Sept. 1809.

THE Commander of the Forces is concerned to hear, that last night, several soldiers came into the town of Badajoz, and plundered a Bakery and the houses of several individuals of bread. This continued misbehaviour of the soldiers gives the Commander of the Forces the greatest concern ; and he is determined, however difficult it may be, to put a stop to it. The rolls are to be called in the different corps of the 4th division every hour till further orders: and the Commander of the Forces desires that no soldier whatever, may be allowed to quit his lines on any account, excepting in charge of an Officer.

The Provost must punish all those found disobeying this order. A guard must be placed at the gate of the town of Badajoz, and all soldiers attempting to pass in are to be made prisoners, and sent to the Provost guard.
The

The Provost will forthwith turn out of the town all soldiers who may be in it.

ADJUTANT GENERAL's OFFICE.
Badajoz, 6th Sept. 1809.

G. O.

CAPTAIN the Hon. H. Pakenham, 95th regiment, is appointed a Deputy Assistant Adjutant General from the 1st instant.

Captain Pakenham is attached to the 3d division until further orders.

ADJUTANT GENERAL's OFFICE.
Badajoz, 7th Sept. 1809.

G. O.

1. NOTWITHSTANDING the repeated orders given out upon the subject, the soldiers of the 4th division of Infantry plundered bee hives, in the neighbourhood of Badajoz, on the day before the division marched from that place; it is impossible these outrages can be committed daily, and that this last outrage in particular could have been committed without the Officers obtaining some knowledge of it. The Officers with the army do not appear to be aware how much they suffer in the disgraceful and unmilitary practices of the soldiers, in marauding and plundering every thing they lay their hands upon. The consequence is, the people of the country fly their habitations, no market is opened, and the Officers, as well as the soldiers, suffer in the privation of every comfort and

every

very necessary, excepting their ration, from the neglect of the former, and the criminal misconduct of the latter. The Commander of the Forces has done, and will continue to do every thing in his power, to put an end to these disgraceful practices; but it is obvious that all his efforts must be fruitless, unless the Officers of the army generally, and individually, exert themselves for the same object.

2. The practice of seizing and detaining carts has been prohibited by the General Orders of the army, but it still continues to such an extent as to render it difficult, if not impossible, to supply the troops with what they require, and if persevered in will again cut off the communications with the sources of supply. Commanding Officers of divisions, brigades, and regiments are referred to the General Orders of the 25th June, No. 10.

3. All carts now with any department, regiment, or individual to which a driver is attached (whether drawn by mules or bullocks) are to be forthwith allowed to return to their homes, the Commissary paying them their hire for the time they have been employed.

4. Regiments or departments which have carts without drivers are to retain them.

5. Commanding Officers of regiments are to report to the Officers commanding brigades, what number of carts with drivers each will have sent away, and what number of carts without drivers each will have retained under these orders. Commanding Officers of brigades will transmit these reports, in the usual channel, to the Quarter-Master General. Heads of departments are to make a similar report to the Quarter-Master General. These orders are not intended to apply to the covered carts drawn by mules lately sent from Seville, nor to any carts actually engaged in

the

the performance of any service, until that service shall have been completed. In future when carts are required by regiments or departments, application is to be made for them to the Commissary General, according to the orders of the 25th of June, No. 10.

6. The Commander of the Forces has observed that camp kettles are, in some instances, carried upon carts, a practice which is positively contrary to orders, and must be exceedingly inconvenient and prejudicial to the troops. He begs that the Officers commanding brigades and regiments wil see that regiments are properly provided with the means of carrying camp kettles without loss of time.

7. The Officer in command of the hospital at Elvas, and the Officer commanding at Lisbon, will take care that every soldier joining the army from either of those places is supplied with two good shirts, and two good pairs of shoes, which will be supplied by the Commissary upon his requisition. The Officer or Non-commissioned Officer, in charge of the hospital of the soldier requiring the necessaries, will make the requisition, specifying in it the soldier's name, the regiment and company to which he belongs, and the number of shirts and pairs of shoes he requires: this must be given in in duplicate; one copy of which must be sent to the regiment, and the other delivered to the Commissary. The Officer or Non-commissioned Officer in charge of the soldier requiring the necessaries, is to sign the receipt of the necessaries at the bottom of both copies of the requisition, when they will have received them from the Commissary.

8. When Officers will be in such a state of health as to render it necessary that they should quit the army, they must send to head quarters a certificate that the state of

their

their health requires removing; this certificate will be sent to the Inspector of hospitals, and a board of Medical Officers will be ordered to assemble to consider of the necessity of this removal; and unless this board should certify that removal is necessary, it will not in any case be permitted. In the same manner, if the medical attendant on any Officer, either with the army or at out-quarter, should think his return to England necessary, he will certify it to the board ordered to consider of the case.

9. At a General Court Marial held at Merida, on the 31st of August, by order of His Excellency Lieutenant General Sir Arthur Wellesley, of which Major General Tilson was President, and Captain Goodman, 48th regiment, Acting Deputy Judge Advocate,—Lieutenant Garland, 91st regiment, and Paymaster of the 1st battalion of detachments, was arraigned for having absented himself from his regiment without leave, at or near Talavera, on or about the 3d August, 1809, and proceeding to the rear without leave; thereby acting in a manner highly prejudicial to good order and military discipline; to which charge, the prisoner pleaded not guilty. The Court proceeded to the examination of witnesses, and having maturely and deliberately weighed and considered the evidence adduced against the prisoner Lieutenant Garland, together with what he has offered in his defence, are of opinion he is not guilty of the first part of the charge preferred against him, viz. for absenting himself from his regiment without leave; it appeared to the Court that he acted under the immediate orders of his Commanding Officer Lieutenant Colonel Banbury: the Court are further of opinion that the prisoner Lieutenant Garland, 91st regiment, is guilty of the latter part of the charge preferred

ferred against him, viz. for having gone to the rear without leave, being a breach of the Articles of War; but it appearing to the Court that he had received no instructions from his Commanding Officer where to find his regiment; and having adduced evidence of his anxiety to join his corps, do only sentence him, the prisoner Lieutenant Garland to be reprimanded at such time and place, and in such manner, as the Commander of the Forces shall think fit. The Commander of the Forces cannot avoid to take this opportunity of observing that when an Officer is separated from his regiment in the performance of his duty, or by unavoidable circumstances, it is his first duty to endeavour to join, when the duty shall have been performed, or the circumstances shall no longer exist which occasioned his separation from his regiment; this is peculiarly his duty, and most probably would be an object to every Officer in this army, at a moment when the army might be supposed to be involved in difficulties. From the excellent character which Lieutenant Garland bears, and from his former services and good conduct, the Commander of the Forces believes with the Court Martial that he was desirous of joining his regiment. That which has occurred to him however, and the fact which is notorious to the whole army, if any effort had been made to join it, it must have been successful, should be a warning to all Officers in the situation in which Lieutenant Garland found himself, not to listen to the senseless reports which invariably prevail on the flank and rear of all armies, but to endeavour seriously to join their regiments; at all events, not to go farther to the rear till the necessity for doing so will have become evident and urgent.

10. It

10. It is directed that particular attention may be paid by the regiments of the army to sending in their weekly states and monthly returns correct. There have been of late so many mistakes and alterations in men and horses unaccounted for, that almost invariably, the states have been returned to the regiments prior to the possibility of making out the general state of the army. This occasions not only trouble, but considerable delay. In addition to the due examination of the returns by the Commanding Officer previous to his signature, and his comparing them with the former to see that they correspond, Brigade Majors and Assistant Adjutant Generals of divisions must strictly compare and examine all states sent in; the latter will be held particularly responsible for forwarding correct states.

12. The General Court Martial of which Major General Tilson was President, is dissolved.

13. A General Court Martial will assemble to-morrow morning, at twelve o'clock.

Lieutenant General Payne, President.

	Brigadier General.	Colonel.	Field Officers.	Captains.
Artillery	1 —	0 —	0 —	1
Cavalry	0 —	0 —	2 —	1
1st Division	0 —	0 —	1 —	1
2d do.	0 —	0 —	2 —	1
4th do.	0 —	1 —	1 —	2
Total .	1 —	1 —	6 —	6

The names of the Officers, and dates of commissions to be sent direct to Captain Goodman, Deputy Judge Advocate, at the Adjutant General's Office.

G. O.

ADJUTANT GENERAL'S OFFICE.

G. O. *Badajoz, 8th Sept.* 1809.

THE Commander of the Forces has heard with much concern, that persons employed at Lisbon in landing stores for the army, have landed goods liable to pay duty, under pretence that they were for the use of the troops. The Commander of the Forces is determined to disgrace and punish those who shall be found out to have been concerned in those scandalous transactions; and in order to prevent them in future, he desires that when any articles are to be landed from any ship in the Tagus for the use of the troops, the Officer at the head of the department, for whose service they are to be landed, is to give one day's previous notice to the Officer commanding at Lisbon, of this intention, stating particularly the ship from which, in the river, and the place to which on shore, the articles are to be taken, and, as far as may be possible, the denominations and quantities of the articles to be landed.

The Commanding Officer at Lisbon is immediately to convey this notice to His Majesty's Ambassador at Lisbon, in order that he may make such communications on the subject to the Government as he may think proper. In case the Government may think proper to order it, Custom-House Officers are to be allowed to attend in the ship, in the boats conveying the articles from the ship to the shore, and in the Store-House, in order to see that the goods are conveyed to their destination according to notice given.

G. A. O.

ADJUTANT GENERAL'S OFFICE.

G. A. O.   *Badajoz, 8th Sept.* 1809.

THE Commander of the Forces desires that the Officers commanding regiments will, as soon as possible after the receipt of this order, send to the Adjutant General a return, stating as far as the regiments have a knowledge, in what hospital the Officers, Non-commissioned Officers, and Soldiers are, who are returned in the weekly states of this day; sick, absent: likewise a return stating where the Officers, Non-commissioned Officers and Soldiers are returned on command in the same state, and a return stating where the men returned, under the column missing, were first missing.

ADJUTANT GENERAL'S OFFICE.

G. O.   *Badajoz, 9th Sept.* 1809.

1. STAFF Surgeons of divisions, Surgeons of brigades, regimental Surgeons, and Assistant Surgeons, having charge of regimental sick, are directed to pay particular attention to the General Orders respecting the hospital department. The Inspector of hospitals has not been able to obtain correct returns of the regimental medical staff and of the sick, from the circumstance of the orders of the 13th August not having been obeyed.

2. Weekly Returns of sick are to be transmitted every Sunday morning to the Inspector of hospitals, and Monthly Returns every 20th, in which will be specified the names of Regimental Surgeons and Assistant Surgeons, whether present or absent, and how employed; also Hospital Mates who may be attached to regiments, must be included in

the

the returns; the general and regimental hospital Staff will transmit to the Inspector of hospitals' head quarters their names, and dates of their commissions from the time of their entrance into the service.

3. The following promotions have taken place in the Hospital Staff.

Apothecary Burnell to be Surgeon to the Forces.

Surgeon John Meade, 40th regiment, do.

Deputy Purveyor William James to be Purveyor to the Forces.

4. The men of the 1st battalion, 42d regiment, and the 1st battalion, 28th regiment, from the battalions of detachments, are to join the 2d battalions of those regiments when the battalions of detachments receive orders to march.

ADJUTANT GENERAL'S OFFICE.

G. O.   *Badajoz, 10th Sept.* 1809.

1. A ROYAL salute to be fired this day, at 1 o'clock, by the artillery at Head Quarters, in honour of the surrender of Flushing, on the 15th August, to His Majesty's troops, under the command of the Earl of Chatham, whereby the conquest of the Island of Walcheren was completed.

2. The Commander of the Forces has much pleasure in publishing to the Officers and troops the following copy of a letter from the Secretary of State, conveying His Majesty's approbation of their gallant conduct in the late action of Talavera.

Downing Street, 21st August, 1809.

Copy of a letter from Viscount Castlereagh, one of His Majesty's principal Secretaries of State, to His Excellency Lieutenant General Sir Arthur Wellesley, K. B.

Sir,

Your letters of the dates referred to in the margin* have been received and laid before the King.

That of the 29th of July, which reports the result of an attack made on the combined British and Spanish armies near Talavera de la Reyna, on the 27th and 28th ult. by the united corps of Victor and Sebastiani, and the troops from Madrid, has been received by His Majesty with the utmost interest and satisfaction.

The nature of the position occupied by the Spanish army, and the deliberate purpose of the enemy to direct his whole efforts against the troops of His Majesty, as it has thrown upon the British army, nearly the entire weight of this great contest, has afforded them an opportunity of acquiring for themselves the important glory of having vanquished the French army of more than double their number, not in a short or partial struggle, but in a battle obstinately contested in two successive days, not wholly discontinued even throughout the intervening night, and fought under circumstances which brought the mass of both armies into close, and repeated combat.

The King in contemplating so glorious a display of the valour and prowess of his troops, has commanded me to declare his royal approbation of the conduct of his whole army.

His Majesty has directed me to signify in the most marked and especial manne to you his gracious sense of

* July 29th.——August 1st.

your

your personal services on the ever-memorable occasion, not less displayed in the glorious result of the battle itself, than in the consummate ability, valour, and military resource with which the many difficulties of this arduous and protracted contest were met, and provided for by your tried experience and judgment.

The conduct of Lieutenant General Sherbrooke has entitled him to the King's entire approbation. His Majesty has observed with satisfaction the manner in which he led on the troops to the charge with the bayonet, a species of attack which, on all occasions, so well accords with the dauntless character of British Soldiers.

His Majesty has noticed with the same gracious approbation, the conduct of the several General and other Officers; all have done their duty, most of them have had occasion of eminently distinguishing themselves; the instances of which, as reported by you, have not escaped His Majesty's attention.

In signifying to the Officers of the army in public orders His Majesty's approbation and thanks, it is His Majesty's pleasure that they be extended in the most distinct and particular manner to the Non-Commissioned Officers and men; on no occasion have they displayed with greater lustre the inestimable qualities which they possess as Soldiers, nor have they on any former occasion, more nobly sustained the military character of the British nation.

In acknowledging the services of the brave army under your command, His Majesty cannot refrain from those expressions of sorrow and regret with which his Royal mind as been affected, at observing the great number of gallant Officers and Soldiers who have fallen at the battle of Talavera.

M 2

His

His paternal feelings derive their best consolation, on this occasion, from the persuasion that bravery so distinguished, and exertions so heroic, cannot but have obtained for their country the most important, and lasting advantages ; and, whilst the security and glory of his own empire has been confirmed by the achievements of his troops. His Majesty trusts that their efforts will not prove unavailing, under Divine Providence, in the defence of the rights and liberties of the Spanish nation.

His Majesty has directed a medal to be distributed to the General and other Officers commanding corps, in commemoration of the victory of Talavera; and has further commanded, that his Royal approbation of the services of his gallant troops in Spain should be published in General Orders to the whole of the British army.

(Signed)   CASTLEREAGH.

ADJUTANT GENERAL's OFFICE.
Badajoz, 11th Sept. 1809.

G. O.

1. PROCEEDINGS of a General Court Martial held under a warrant from Sir Arthur Wellesley, K. B. bearing date Merida, 26th August, 1809, of which Brigadier General C. Crawford is President, and Captain F. Cockburne, 60th regiment, Deputy Judge Advocate.—The Court proceeded to the trial of Private John Henry, of the 28th regiment, for the wilful murder of a Portuguese inhabitant, on or about the 16th ult. The prisoner pleaded not guilty, and the Court proceeded to the examination of evidences, and having maturely and deliberately considered the evidence produced in support of the charge, as well as the evidence produced in his defence, are of opinion that

the

the Portuguese was killed by the shot fired by private John Henry, of the 28th regiment, but do acquit him of the crime laid to his charge, viz. for wilfully murdering a Portuguese inhabitant, and as much as it appeared to the Court that the said private John Henry, of the 28th regiment, acted under the impression of having received orders and without any malicious intention, and do therefore acquit him accordingly; which sentence has been confirmed by Lieutenant General Sir Arthur Wellesley.

The Court next proceeded to the trial of Serjeants Joseph Dale and William Wright, of the 28th regiment, for unsoldierlike conduct, on the 16th ult., in attempting to press two mules from a Portuguese inhabitant without due authority for so doing, and for ordering one or more soldiers of the guard under their command to fire, by which means the Portuguese lost his life: the prisoners pleaded not guilty, and the Court proceeded to the examination of witnesses, and having maturely and deliberately considered the evidences against the prisoners, as well as what was offered in their defence, are of opinion that they are guilty of unsoldierlike conduct, in having attempted, on or about the 16th ult. to press two mules from a Portuguese inhabitant without due authority; and that they are guilty of authorising the guard to fire. The Court do acquit the prisoners of ordering the guard to fire. The Court do sentence the prisoners, Serjeant Joseph Dale, and Serjeant William Wright, to be reduced to the ranks, and to receive a punishment of 800 lashes each, at such time and at such place as His Excellency the Commander of the Forces may be pleased to appoint.

The Commander of the Forces, in consequence of the recommendation of the Court Martial, pardons the pri-

                                soners,

soners, Serjeant Dale, and Serjeant Wright; they are to be released from their arrest and to return to their duty as Serjeants, in the 2d battalion, 28th regiment.

2. The Commander of the Forces cannot however avoid to observe that unfortunate catastrophe which has occurred, and the circumstances which have brought these Serjeants to trial before the General Court Martial originated in disobedience of orders, repeatedly given out in orders.

3. The use and object of a Sick-Cart to any regiment is to carry the men, or the arms of the men who may be taken ill on the march; and in order to accomplish this object, the cart ought to be with the regiment, and not two days march in the rear: if a cart is to be employed to carry sick men, it should equally accompany the regiment, in which case, if the cattle which draw it should be tired, application might be made to the Commissary for fresh cattle, and at all events, no cart carrying sick should be left without some Medical Officer attending it: besides this, the Commander of the Forces observes, that the Paymaster's books, and probably other articles belonging to him were left upon this cart, which is positively contrary to orders, other means being provided to carry the Paymaster's books; and he desires that the Commanding Officer of the 2d battalion, 28th regiment, will call on the Paymaster to account for his books being upon this cart, and will report whether he is now furnished with a horse, or mule, to carry his books.

4. The occurrences which have been the subject, and have been brought out before this General Court Martial, pointed out forcibly the necessity that the Officers of the army should obey strictly the orders they receive.

5. The

5. The means of transport and conveyance are so scarce in this country, that unless the regulations respecting them are strictly obeyed, the army cannot be served; and most particularly it cannot be served if every officer, and Non-commissioned Officer is to do as he pleases, and take what he pleases by force of arms, wherever he may meet it.

9. Lieutenant Hoey, 18th Hussars, is appointed Aide-de-Camp to Brigadier General the Hon. Charles Stewart, vice Lieutenant George Fitzclarence, who has received the Commander of the Forces' leave of absence to return to England for the recovery of his health.

10. Assistant Provost Marshal Boyle is dismissed from his situation, by the Commander of the Forces, and to return to his regimental duty, for neglect of duty.

G. A. O.　　　　　**ADJUTANT GENERAL's OFFICE.**
Badajoz, 12th Sept. 1809.

THE 4th division having again in three instances plundered bee-hives, notwithstanding the orders of the 7th instant, the regiments of that division are forthwith, upon the receipt of this order, to be turned out and placed under arms, and they are not to quit their arms till one hour after sun-set, when they are to be sent to their huts, and sentries placed round the camp to prevent all men from straggling; and they are to be put under arms again to-morrow morning, at an hour before sun-rise, and to stand by their arms till an hour after sun-set, and so on day after day, till the soldiers shall have been discovered who have been guilty of these outrages, which it is repeated, cannot be committed without the knowledge of the Officers and

Non-

Non-commissioned Officers of the regiments. When the regiments shall be under arms, men must be sent on fatigue for water, for their provisions to cook, &c. &c. under charge of Officers and Non-commissioned Officers, in proportion to the strength of the parties, who must be brought back to the lines as soon as the work required for them shall have been performed.

Colonel Kemmis will report whether the orders of the 4th instant, requiring thàt the rolls should be called in the 4th division every hour, have been obeyed. This order is not intended to apply to the 11th regiment.

ADJUTANT GENERAL'S OFFICE.
Badajoz, 13th Sept. 1809.

G. O.

1. SERJEANT Blackwell, of the 40th regiment, is appointed Assistant Provost, and is attached to the 4th division until further orders.

ADJUTANT GENERAL'S OFFICE.
Badajoz, 14th Sept. 1809.

G. O.

1. THE orders of the 12th instant respecting the plunder of bee-hives by the troops of the 4th division, are countermanded; the plunderers having been discovered and ordered for trial.

2. The Commander of the Forces is always concerned when he is obliged to order any measure of severity towards the troops; he is concerned that the disorders of which frequent complaints are made, are committed by a few; but unless the good soldiers and the Officers and

Non-

Non-commissioned Officers in particular, exert themselves to prevent these outrages, and discover the perpetrators when they are known to them, the whole army must suffer in character, as well as the privations which are the invariable consequence of plunder by the troops.

3. The cavalry have been distributed in their present quarters, principally with a view to their being fed with facility, and in order that the horses might recover their condition. In order to insure this object, it is desirable that they may not be used as orderlies to carry letters, and the Commander of the Forces prefers infinitely to pay for messengers to the use of the cavalry in this manner.

If it should be necessary however, at any time to send a dragoon with a letter, in consequence of the impossibility of procuring a messenger, the Commander of the Forces desires that his rate may be confined to the walk of his horse, unless in a case of very urgent necessity which may require the early delivery of the letter.

4. The Commander of the Forces being desirous of receiving a report of the exact state of health of the Officers sick at Elvas, requests Dr. Frank to go over there, and to visit each of them, and converse with the medical Officer who attends them, and report at what time it is probable each will be enabled to return to his duty.

5. The Non-commissioned Officers and Soldiers belonging to the 5th, 28th, 42d, 43d, 52d, and 95th, in the battalions of detachments, are to be sent to join the battalions of their regiments respectively, now in Spain and Portugal. The men's accounts are to be settled, and their balances paid to the 24th August, and the Officers commanding their companies in the battalions of detachments, will hand over to the Officer appointed to receive the men

in

in the regiments to which the men belong, their subsistence to the 24th September, and the state of their accounts.

6. The men in hospital and on command, belonging to the battalions of detachments of those regiments respectively, are likewise to be transferred to the battalion of their regiment serving in Spain and Portugal, and to be accounted for in their returns; and the Officers commanding their companies in the battalions of detachments, will hand over to the Officers appointed to receive them, the accounts of the men belonging to the regiments above mentioned, who are in hospital and on command.

ADJUTANT GENERAL'S OFFICE.
Badajoz, 15th Sept. 1809.

G. O.

1. THE Rev. Mr. Scott, Brigade Chaplain to the army, being arrived, is to be considered as a Brigade Chaplain, attached to the army in Portugal and Spain, from the 3d of May, 1809.

The Rev. Mr. Scott is to be attached to General Sherbrook's division of Infantry, and will join it to-morrow.

ADJUTANT GENERAL'S OFFICE.
Badajoz, 16th Sept. 1809.

G. O.

PROCEEDINGS of a General Court Martial, held under a warrant of Lieutenant General Sir Arthur Wellesley, K. B. bearing date Badajoz, 9th Sept. 1809, of which Lieutenant General Payne is President, and Captain Goodman Deputy Judge Advocate. The Court proceeded to the trial of Major Nigel Kingscote, 53d regiment, arraigned on the following charges, viz.

1st, For

1st, For not using the necessary exertions for furthering the public service, and for not executing his duty as Major of the 53d regiment, by allowing a Subaltern Officer to remain a night in his tent, while the said Subaltern was on guard; conniving by that means at the non-execution of his (Lieutenant Beatty's) duty, to the prejudice of good order and military discipline, in affording a bad example to the rest of the Officers of the regiment.

2d, For absenting himself from the division during the whole or greater part of the march, on the morning of the 10th of August, and affording more particularly at that period, a bad example to the junior Officers of the regiment, one of whom, Lieutenant Beatty, he allowed to accompany him during the time he was absent.

To which charges, the prisoner pleaded not guilty, and the Court proceeded to the examination of witnesses, and came to the following opinion.

The Court having maturely weighed and considered the evidence adduced in the prosecution against the prisoner Major Nigel Kingscote, 53d regiment, together with what he has alleged in his defence and the evidence thereon, are of opinion he is not guilty of the charges preferred against him, and do therefore fully acquit him of the same. The Court think it necessary to observe, that although Major Kingscote was for a short time absent, during the march of the 10th of August, there appears no criminality attached to it, as he, Major Kingscote, used every possible exertion on the preceding night to find out the hour of march for the regiment, and every effort to join it the following morning after it had marched.

Which sentence is confirmed by his Excellency the Commander of the Forces.

1. The

1. The Commander of the Forces cannot avoid to take this opportunity of calling upon the Field Officers of the regiments in particular, and all the Officers in general, to support and assist their Commanding Officer in the maintenance of discipline, and in the preservation of order and regularity in their corps.

2. The Officers of the army are much mistaken if they suppose that their duty is done when they have attended to the drill of their men, and to the parade duties of the regiment: the order and regularity of the troops in camp and quarters; the subsistence and comfort of the soldiers, the general subordination and obedience of the corps afford constant subjects for the attention of the Field Officers in particular, in which, by their conduct in the assistance they will give their Commanding Officer, they can manifest their zeal for the service, their ability and their fitness for promotion to the higher ranks, at least equally as by an attention to the drill and parade discipline of the corps.

3. The Commander of the Forces desires that the principle of the order of the 29th May, given out at Coimbra, which requires that Officers should be quartered near the companies, may be applied to the encampments, that the tents of the Officers may be placed near those of the men under their command, and that the situations of the Field Officers may be pitched-upon by the Quarter-Master of the battalion.

Proceedings of a General Court Martial, held under a warrant from Lieutenant General Sir A. Wellesley K. B. bearing date Badajoz, 13th Sept. 1809, of which Lieutenant General Payne is President, and Captain Goodman Deputy Judge Advocate.

The

The Court proceeded to the trial of Lieutenant Lynch, of the Queen's regiment, for striking a Portuguese sentry at Elvas, on the 4th Sept. 1809, taking his bayonet forcibly from him, and throwing it away, &c. to which charge the prisoner pleaded not guilty; and the Court proceeded to the examination of evidences, and having maturely weighed the evidence produced in support of the charges, with what the prisoner had to say in his defence, are of opinion there is not sufficient evidence to substantiate the charges preferred against him; and do therefore acquit the prisoner; which sentence has been cofirmed by the Commander of the Forces.

4. The Commander of the Forces desires that all Officers and Soldiers of the army will understand, that the Spanish and Portuguese soldiers are entrusted with the performance of duties when sentry, equally with British soldiers in the same situation; and that any resistance to a Spanish or Portuguese sentry, and particularly any violence committed upon him, upon any assumed superiority of character, by any British Officer or soldier, will be punished as such a breach of military discipline shall deserve.

5. Return of 165 days forage money to be sent in to the Quarter-Master General's immediately.

6. Lieutenant A. Weyland, 16th Light Dragoons, is appointed Aide-de-Camp to Brigadier General Anson, in the absence of Captain Pelly, to bear date 12th Sept. 1809.

7. A General Court Martial will assemble on Monday, the 18th instant, at Badajoz, of which Major General Cotton will be President.

Detail

Detail for the General Court Martial ordered to as-
semble at Budajoz, on Monday the 18th instant.

	Field Officers.	Captains.	Subalterns.
Divisions of Cavalry	0	1	0
1st do. of Infantry	1	1	1
2d do. of do.	1	2	1
3d do. of do.	1	1	1
4th do. of do.	1	1	1
Total . . .	4	6	4

ADJUTANT GENERAL's OFFICE.
G. O.   *Badajoz, 17th Sept.* 1809.

1. THE Officers commanding the battalions of detachments, will report to the Adjutant General, when they
have carried into execution the orders of the 14th instant,
No. 5, in which report they will specify the numbers of
men transferred to each of the regiments enumerated in
that order.

2. The General Court Martial of which Lieutenant
General Payne is President, is dissolved, and the members
are to return to their duty.

3. Officers who require quarters at any of the stations of
the army, or at head-quarters, are to apply to the Officer
of the Quarter-Master General's department at such stations, or to Captain Kelly, at head-quarters, for billets,
and are not on any account to apply themselves to the Magistrates. Captain Kelly, at head-quarters, and the Officers of the Quarter-Master General's department, at the
                                                    other

other stations of the army, will keep a register of the
names of the Officers for whom they procure billets, stating the name of the owner of the house on whom the billet
is procured, so that it may always be known what Officers
have been quartered in each house.

5. The Hon. Lieutenant Colonel Pakenham will proceed to Abrantes, and take charge of the brigade of Infantry, hitherto under the command of Major General
Lightburne, during that Officer's absence on account of
indisposition.

G. A. O. *Badajoz, 17th Sept. 1809.*

In consequence of the indisposition of Major General
Cotton, Brigadier General Anson will be President of the
General Court Martial ordered to assemble to-morrow
morning.

G. O. ADJUTANT GENERAL's OFFICE.
Badajoz, 19th Sept. 1809.

At a General Court Martial held at Badajoz, by order
of His Excellency Sir Arthur Wellesley, of which Lieutenant General Payne was President, and Captain Goodman Deputy Judge Advocate—The Court proceeded to
the trial of James Hillon and Michael Dobs, 28th regiment, John Cany, 31st regiment, William Stubbins, 34th,
Thomas Caine, 53d, John Miggins, 87th, Michael Kiggan,

gan, 87th, William O'Brian, 88th, Louis Bincker, King's German Legion, arraigned on the following charges, viz.

For plundering His Majesty's stores of Shoes while on an escort from Lisbon with the said stores; to which the prisoners pleaded not guilty, and the Court proceeded to the examination of witnesses; and having maturely and deliberately weighed and considered the evidence adduced on the prosecution against the prisoners, together with what they have alleged in their defence, and the evidence thereon, are of opinion, they are each and every one of them guilty of the charge preferred against them, being a breach of the Articles of War; and by virtue thereof, sentence them to receive a punishment of 500 lashes each, at such time and place, and iu such manner as the Commander of the Forces shall deem fit: which sentence has been confirmed by His Excellency the Commander of the Forces.

2. The prisoners, William Stubbins, of the 34th regiment, and Louis Binckar, of the King's German Legion, are pardoned, in consequence of the recommendation of the General Court Martial, and are to be released from confinement and sent to their regiments. The other prisoners are to be sent to join their corps, where the punishment sentenced by the Court is to be inflicted on them, in presence of the regiments to which they belong, under arms, and one company from each of the other regiments cantoned in the same place.

3. John Miggins and Michael Kiggan, of the 87th regiment, are to receive their punishment from the drummers of the 88th regiment, and are afterwards to be sent to the hospital at Elvas.

4. The Commander of the Forces cannot avoid to take this opportunity of drawing the attention of the army to

the

the unworthy conduct of these soldiers, who have plundered the stores on their way to the army, for the use of their
comrades, over which they were placed as a guard.

———————

G. O.

ADJUTANT GENERAL's OFFICE.
Badajoz, 21st Sept. 1809.

1. WHEN regimental hospitals are to be established in
any division of the army, they must be formed in the manner pointed out in his Majesty's Regulations ; and the soldiers who go into regimental hospitals must be under a
stoppage of 9d. per diem, which must be paid to the Regimental Surgeon, or other person in charge of the hospital, and accounted for in conformity with those regulations.

2. This stoppage is intended to enable the Surgeon to
subsist the soldier in regimental hospital, as well as to
provide him with those comforts which his situation will
require ; but as it may happen, that the divisions may be
placed in situations in which there is no market, and the
Surgeons of Regiments would find it impracticable to purchase food for the soldiers in hospital; General Officers
commanding divisions are in such case requested to order
the Commissaries attached to their divisions, to supply
the Regimental Surgeons with such proportion of a ration for each man in hospital as they may think proper,
for which Regimental Surgeons will make a daily requisition on the Commissary ; and the Regimental Surgeons
are to pay for each of these rations such proportion of 6d.
as that they will receive will bear to the whole ration of
the soldier.

3. These sums are to be paid to the Commissary, and the account closed by the Regimental Surgeons, on the 25th of every month, for all that he will have received from the 25th of the preceding month, to the 24th of the current month.

4. The Soldiers are to pay six shillings for each pair of shoes received from the Commissary General, and six shillings and seven pence for each shirt. The Commissary General will make known to the Paymaster General as soon as possible, what number of each have been delivered to each regiment, in order that the price may be stopped from the regiment, and the soldiers may pay for them in the muster ending on the 24th instant.

5. Captain Backmeister having acted as Brigade Major to the brigade of Hanoverian Legion, is to be paid as Brigade Major from the period in which he was appointed to act in that situation.

Memorandum—The Rev. Mr. Allott is attached to the 2d division of the army, and is to report himself to Major General Hill.

———————————

ADJUTANT GENERAL'S OFFICE.
Badajoz, 21st Sept. 1809.

G. A. O.

AT a General Court Martial, held by order of his Excellency Lieutenant General Lord Wellington, of which Brigadier General Anson was President, and Captain Goodman Deputy Judge Advocate—The Court proceeded to the trial of Robert Costello, private in the corps of Royal Military Artificers, arraigned for wilful murder, in stabbing and wounding private George Spratt, of the

same

same corps at Badajoz, on the 13th September, 1809, of which wound, or wounds, he, the said George Spratt, died on the following day; to which charge the prisoner pleaded not guilty, and the Court proceeded to the examination of witnesses, and having considered with mature deliberation the evidence adduced on the prosecution against the prisoner, Robert Costello, private in the corps of Royal Military Artificers, together with what he has offered in his defence, are of opinion he is not guilty of the charge preferred against him, and do therefore acquit him of the same.

Which sentence has been approved of by his Excellency the Commander of the Forces.

———————————

ADJUTANT GENERAL'S OFFICE.
Badajoz, 22d Sept. 1809.

G. O.

1. AT a General Court Martial held by order of Lieutenant General Lord Viscount Wellington at Badajoz, of which Brigadier General Anson was President, and Captain Goodman Deputy Judge Advocate—The Court proceeded to the trial of privates Antony Moore, William Mitchell, and James Murphey, 53d regiment, arraigned for plundering bee-hives, on or about the evening of the 12th instant; to which the prisoners pleaded not guilty, and the Court proceeded to the examination of witnesses, and having considered the evidence adduced on the prosecution against the prisoners Anthony Moore, William Mitchell, and James Murphey, privates in the 53d regiment, together with what they have offered in their defence, are of opinion they are guilty of the charge preferred against

N 2

them,

them, being a breach of the Articles of War, and do by virtue thereof, sentence the prisoners Anthony Moore, and William Mitchell, 53d regiment, to receive a punishment of 700 lashes each; and the prisoner James Murphey, a punishment of 500 lashes, at such time and place, and in such manner as the Commander of the Forces may deem fit.

Which sentence has been confirmed by his Excellency the Commander of the Forces.

2. The prisoners are to be sent forthwith to the 4th division, where the sentence of the General Court Martial is to be carried into execution, in presence of the 53d regiment under arms, and one company from each of the other regiments of the division. The Commanding Officer of the 4th division will give directions respecting the time and place at which the punishment will be carried into execution.

3. The Commander of the Forces cannot avoid to express his regret upon losing the services of the two battalions of detachments, which are about to join their corps in England; he will not flatter them by saying that he has not had, upon several occasions, reasons to be dissatisfied with their conduct, in their quarters, their camps, and on their marches; but they have uniformly sustained, in an exemplary manner, the character of the regiments to which they belong, and of Britsih Soldiers, in the field against the enemy; and he trusts that the few, of whose conduct he cannot but complain, even upon this occasion, will discontinue and forget their bad practices and habits, upon their return to their regiments; and that they will endeavour to become an example of orderly, and regular conduct in their quarters, as they must ever be of gallantry

and

and discipline in the field. He requests Lieutenant Colonel Banbury, Lieutenant Colonel Copson, and the Officers attached to these battalions, to accept his acknowledgement for the attention they have given to them.

4. As it has appeared, to the satisfaction of the Commander of the Forces, that Captain Henry Dickens has been promoted to be Major of the 34th regiment; he is to join and do duty as Major with the 2d battalion of that regiment.

5. The 3d battalion, 27th regiment, is to join the army as soon as relieved by the 2d battalion, 87th regiment, according to routes to be furnished by the Quarter-Master General, and this corps is to join and form part of the brigade under the command of Colonel Kemmis.

ADJUTANT GENERAL's OFFICE.
Badajoz, 23d Sept. 1809.

G. O.

1. AT a General Court Martial held at Badajoz, by order of Lieutenant General Lord Viscount Wellington, of which Brigadier General Anson was President, and Captain Goodman Deputy Judge Advocate, the Court proceeded to the trial of private William Harding, 52d regiment, arraigned for desertion, on or about the 6th of June 1809, and not returning until brought back by an escort to the Provost Guard, on or about the 16th August; to which charge the prisoner pleaded not guilty, and the Court proceeded to the examination of witnesses, and having considered, with mature deliberation, the evidence adduced on the prosecution against the prisoner William Harding, private in the 52d regiment, together with what he has offered in his defence and the evidence thereon, are

of

of opinion he is not guilty of the charge preferred against him, and do therefore acquit the prisoner William Harding, private in the 52d regiment, of the same; which sentence has been confirmed by his Excellency the Commander of the Forces.

2. All claims for losses, whether personal or regimental, must be sent in to the Military Secretary of the Commander of the Forces, without loss of time, accompanied by a statement of the circumstances by which each was occasioned, and of the proof by which the loss and its causes can be substantiated.

3. The Paymasters of the regiments of the 1st and 4th divisions of the army will, on to-morrow, receive from the Paymaster General, the balances of their estimates from the 25th August, to the 24th September, and the Paymasters of the 2d and 3d divisions on the 25th instant, and the Paymasters of the cavalry on the 26th.

5. Of the three returns of 165 days forage money sent in by the regiments to the Quarter-Master General's Office, one will be sent back to the regiments after being examined, which must be given in to the Commissary General, when payment of the amount is claimed by the regimental Paymaster.

> 6. *Copy of a Letter from Sir David Dundas, K. B. Commander in Chief, to Lieutenant General Sir A. Wellesley.*

(CIRCULAR.)   Horse Guards,
17th July, 1809.

Sir,

Referring to my letter of the 6th ult. transmitting printed regulations respecting the bât. and forage
money

money of the army—I have to acquaint you, for your further information and guidance, that the Lords Commissioners of his Majesty's Treasury, in directing that particular attention may be paid to those, and other regulations, laid down by the Treasury Board, have desired that it may be distinctly understood, that the baggage and bât money should in no case be issued more than once in any one year to troops going, or being on foreign service, or for more than 365 days, should not take place except under very special circumstances, until the expiration of ninety days at least, after the issue of the first.

Their Lordships approve that the allowance to troops taking the field at home, should continue under the existing regulations, and in the event of embarkation, the difference, if any, is to be made good to the Officer embarking.

A misconception having arisen on some occasions, when troops were ordered to embark, that they are entitled to an allowance under the description of Embarkation Money; it is to be understood in the army that the bât and baggage money, and the allowance for 200 days forage will be issued, henceforward, to the troops before they embark for foreign service, unless they shall have previously received it within the same year, and that no other allowance is forth-coming on that occasion, except in cases of promotion, when the difference will be issued in conformity to the regulations laid down by the Board of General Officers.

(Signed)   **DAVID DUNDAS,**

Commander in Chief.

ADJUTANT GENERAL'S OFFICE.

G. A. O. *Badajoz, 24th Sept.* 1809.

THE Order of this day, respecting the Paymasters coming to Head-Quarters to receive the balance of their estimates, is suspended.

ADJUTANT GENERAL'S OFFICE.

G. O. *Badajoz, 24th Sept.* 1809.

1. THE mistakes made in the Returns and States sent from many of the regiments of the army are so frequent, and so glaring, that the Commander of the Forces apprehends that the proper mode of keeping an account of their men is neglected, or is not known in those regiments. The foundation of all states and returns is the roll, and morning and evening states of the troop or company, in which every man absent ought to be accounted for by name, including casualties, till struck off the strength by order of the Commanding Officer of the regiment.

The weekly and other states called for from regiments are made up of the totals of the states of each troop or company, which totals should be entered in the regimental weekly or monthly State Book, and at the bottom the names of all men making any alteration from the preceding state, should be entered by companies.

2. No state should be ever sent in without being made to tally with the last state sent in, and it may be certain that if the second state, whether weekly or monthly, does not account for every man returned in the first, there has

been

been an error, which ought to be investigated, and rectified before the state is sent in.

3. These orders have been called for, principally by the manner in which the After General Order of the 8th September, requiring the regiments to account in detail for the men returned by each on command, in the weekly state sent to the Adjutant General on the 8th instant, has been obeyed by many of the regiments, particularly by the 2d battalion 87th Regiment, and 1st battalion 88th Regiment.

4. The Commander of the Forces is convinced that either those regiments have never known the proper mode of making out a return, or that their interior economy has been lately entirely neglected.

5. He requests the General Officers commanding brigades to inspect accurately the books of the regiments of their brigades, and to see in what manner they make out their states, whether the absent men of each troop or company are accurately accounted for by name on the rolls, and on the morning and evening states at every parade, and that they will look particularly into the interior economy of the regiments under their command.

6. The Commander of the Forces wishes the Commanding and other Officers of the regiments, particularly the Field Officers, to recollect that there is a great deal to do to keep their regiments in order upon service, besides attending to the parades and drills of the men.

7. The Commander of the Forces desires that Colonel Peacock will pay attention to the state of discipline (meaning by that word habits of obedience to orders, subordination, regularity, and interior economy) of the 2d battalion 83d Regiment, and 2d battalion 87th Regiment,

lately

lately ordered to Lisbon, as well as to their parade discipline and drill.

8. The Commander of the Forces deems it but justice to the two battalions of Guards to state that their returns have in every respect been as accurate as the conduct of these excellent corps have been regular and exemplary in every other respect.

The returns of the Legion and of the regiments of Cavalry are also very accurate.

Memorandum. — Surgeon M'Gilivray, 5th battalion 60th, is appointed to act as Surgeon to the 31st Regiment, vice Dire, deceased, until his Majesty's pleasure is known.

Assistant Surgeon Van Millenger, 97th Regiment, is appointed to act as Surgeon to the 5th battalion 60th, vice M'Gilivray.

ADJUTANT GENERAL'S OFFICE,
Badajoz, 26th Sept. 1809.

G. O.

1. AT a General Court Martial held in pursuance of an order from his Excellency the Right Honourable Lord Viscount Wellington, K. B. Commander of the Forces, of which Brigadier General Anson was President, and Captain Goodman, Deputy Judge Advocate—The Court being duly sworn proceeded to the trial of Marcus Dalhunty, Esq. Paymaster 1st battalion 45th Regiment, arraigned for absenting himself from his regiment without leave, at or near Talavera, on or about the 3d of August, 1809, and proceeding to the rear without leave, thereby acting in a manner highly prejudicial to good order and military

military discipline, to which charge the prisoner pleaded *not guilty*, and the Court proceeded to the examination of witnesses, and having maturely and deliberately weighed and considered the evidence adduced on the prosecution against the prisoner, Marcus Dalhunty, Esq. Paymaster 1st battalion 45th Regiment, together with what he has alleged in his defence, and the evidence thereon, are of opinion he is not guilty of the first part of the charge preferred against him, viz. for absenting himself from his regiment without leave, at or near Talavera, on or about the 3d of August, 1809; it appearing to the Court that he was sanctioned in so doing by his Commanding Officer, and do therefore acquit him of the same. The Court are farther of opinion that the prisoner, Marcus Dalhunty, Esq. Paymaster of the 1st battalion 45th Regiment, is guilty of the latter part of the charge preferred against him, viz. for proceeding to the rear without leave, being a breach of the Articles of War, and do by virtue thereof sentence him to be reprimanded by his Commanding Officer, in presence of the Officers of the 45th Regiment, at such time and place as his Excellency the Commander of the Forces may appoint. The Court are induced to award this lenient sentence, from the peculiar circumstance under which the prisoner was placed; which sentence has been confirmed by his Excellency the Commander of the Forces.

2. The Commander of the Forces refers the Officers of the Medical Staff to the General Orders of the 7th September, (No. 8.) in which they will find detailed the mode in which Medical Boards must be ordered, and the certificates by which it must be preceded. He will notice

tice no reports of Medical Boards that are not held in conformity with the mode pointed out in that order.

ADJUTANT GENERAL's OFFICE.
G. O.   *Badajoz, 27th Sept.* 1809.

1. CAPTAIN Robert Maunsell, 39th Regiment, is to act as Brigade Major to the brigade of Infantry under the command of Brigadier General Catlin Crawford, vice Dickens, promoted.

2. Serjeant-Major Dixon, 2d battalion 58th, is appointed to act as Adjutant to the 2d battalion 48th, vice Peacocke, deceased.

ADJUTANT GENERAL's OFFICE.
G. O.   *Badajoz, 29th Sept.* 1809.

THE following Officers have been appointed to serve on the Staff in the army serving in Spain and Portugal.

Brigadier General John Slade, dated 17th August; Aide-de-Camp Lieutenant Eckersley, 1st or Royal Regiment of Dragoons, Brigade Major.

ADJUTANT GENERAL's OFFICE.
G. O.   *Badajoz, 1st Oct.* 1809.

1. THE Commander of the Forces observes that the women of the regiments have come up from Lisbon along
with

with the clothing, to the great inconvenience of the army, and to their own detriment; and as they travel on the cars, they delay and render uncertain the arrival of the regimental clothing for the troops, and defeat all the arrangements for bringing it up to the army.

2. The Commander of the Forces desires that Colonel Peacocke will prevent the women from leaving Lisbon with the clothing and regimental baggage; and the Officers and Non-commissioned Officers coming up from Lisbon in charge of clothing are desired to prevent the women from travelling on the carts.

3. The Order, No. 3, of the 23d September, is to be carried into execution to-morrow and the following days, by the Paymasters of regiments.

———————

G. O.

ADJUTANT GENERAL'S OFFICE.
Badajoz, 2d Oct. 1809.

. A GENERAL Court Martial will assemble at Badajoz, on Wednesday, the 4th Instant, at 11 o'Clock, for the trial of such prisoners as may be brought before it.

President, Brigadier General R. Crawford.

	Field Officers.	Captains.	Subalterns.
Division of Cavalry	0	1	1
1st Division of Infantry	1	1	1
2d ditto	1	2	0
3d ditto	1	1	1
4th ditto	1	1	1
Total	4	6	4

Member

Members names and dates of commissions to be sent in to the Adjutant General's Office immediately, directed to the Deputy Judge Advocate.

All evidences to be warned and to attend.

2. *The following Letter has been received from the Horse Guards.*

(Copy.)

HORSE GUARDS.
31st *August*, 1809.

MY LORD,

I HAVE received the Commander in Chief's command to acquaint your Lordship that his Majesty has been pleased to approve of Major Generals Cotton and Hill serving in Spain and Portugal being placed on the Staff of the Army as Lieutenant Generals, during the continuance of that service only.

I have, &c.

To Lieutenant General   (Signed)   J. W. GORDON.
Lord Wellington.

ADJUTANT GENERAL'S OFFICE.
Badajoz, 4th Oct. 1809.

G. O.

LIEUTENANT the Honourable R. Quinn, 44th Regiment, is appointed Aide-de-Camp to Lieutenant General Payne.

G. O.

G. O.　　　　　Adjutant General's Office,
　　　　　　　　　Badajoz, 6th Oct. 1809.

As it is understood that several Officers of the army have found, and have now in their possession, saddles and other horse appointments belonging to the regiments of Cavalry, the Commander of the Forces requests that the Commanding Officers of regiments and Heads of Departments will make inquiries respecting these appointments, and make a return to the Quarter-Master General of the names of such Officers as are willing to return them to the regiments to which they belonged. The Commanding Officers of those regiments returning to those individuals articles of the same description of the manufacture of Portugal or Spain.

Memorandum.—The following promotions in the Medical Department have been notified from England.

Surgeon William Wallace, 7th Foot.

————————————Brough, 83d Foot.

Deputy Purveyor Maypother to be Surgeon to the Forces.

The following Gentlemen are appointed to act by the Commander of the Forces until his Majesty's pleasure is known.

Assistant Surgeon Williamson, 28th Regiment, to be Surgeon to the 7th Foot, vice Wallace.

Assistant Surgeon Forcade, 40th Regiment, to be Surgeon to 83d, vice Brough.

Hospital Mate Booty, to be Assistant Surgeon to the 97th, vice Van Millinger.

Hospital

Hospital Mate Barry, to be Assistant Surgeon to the 40th, vice Forcade.

Hospital Mate Ivory, to be Assistant Surgeon to the 3d or Buffs, vice Aire.

Hospital Mate Weadon, to be Apothecary to the Forces, vice Graham, deceased.

ADJUTANT GENERAL's OFFICE.
Badajoz, 7th Oct. 1809.

G. O.

1. A BOARD of Claims is to be assembled at Campo Mayor, consisting of Brigadier General R. Crawford, Lieutenant Colonel Beckwith, Lieutenant Colonel Gifford, Major Arbuthnot, and Major Stewart, for the consideration and decision of all claims of Officers and Soldiers of the army, for losses sustained up to the 1st October.

The claims sent to the Military Secretary will be referred to this Board for their consideration and decision.

2. The principles on which such claims are to be considered and decided are as follows : no claim for a loss can be allowed, which has been occasioned by a disobedience of orders, or by neglect or omission in the party claiming for the loss, or his servant or bât men.

No claim can be allowed for a loss sustained by the ordinary occurrences of the service, such as deaths of horses or mules of fatigue, occasioned by the ordinary marches of the army, the loss of accoutrements and necessaries

cessaries in hospital, or by the breaking down of carts, fatigue of oxen, &c. &c.

3. As the principle on which the compensation for losses by the public is founded, is that the claimant may replace his loss, and the public may not lose his services ; claims for losses on behalf of Officers or Soldiers who are dead cannot be admitted.

4. As the Officers of the army have been restricted in the amount of their baggage by different orders by the late and by the present Commander of the Forces, it would be inconsistent with every principle on which compensation for losses is granted, and with the practice of former Boards of Claims, if the full amount of the value of the whole of an Officer's baggage (as allowed by his Majesty's regulations) was granted to replace the baggage allowed to be carried, or actually carried by any Officer on the service, in Spain or Portugal.

5. The value of the whole and of the different proportions of Officers' baggage lost, is to be rated at two-thirds of the sum allowed by his Majesty's regulations.

6. The claim for regimental baggage, accoutrements, and horse appointments lost, are likewise to be considered as decided upon by the Board upon the same principles.

7. But it is to be observed that clothing, accoutrements, and horse appointments lost, can be paid for according to the practice of the service, only when they shall be replaced by new, and then only three-fourths of the price.

8. The Commander of the Forces is concerned to be obliged to notice that, notwithstanding repeated orders upon the subject, and particularly the General Order of

the 4th of May, the Officers of the army continue to give receipts for articles of provisions and forage, notwithstanding that other arrangements are made for their supply.

9. Those Officers marching up from Lisbon, in particular, either alone or with detachments, have taken up articles of provisions and forage upon their own receipts, contrary to the orders given them in their routes, and notwithstanding that there is a Commissary at every stage, at which it is specified in their route that they are to receive the provisions and forage for themselves and their detachments.

10. This repeated disobedience of all order defeats every arrangement which can be made for the regular supply of the troops, and gives the Commander of the Forces the greatest concern. He is determined to carry into execution his Order of the 4th May, and he gives notice that every Officer who shall make a requisition, and give a receipt for any article of supply, will be called upon to account for his having done so; and if his act should have been in disobedience of orders, or unnecessary, such Officer will have to pay for the supplies for which he will have given a receipt.

11. In case any Officer or Non-commissioned Officer should have occasion to make a requisition and sign a receipt for any article of supply delivered by any of the Magistrates of the country, the requisition and receipt must be made out according to the following Form, and can always be procured in print from any of the Commissaries.

FORM.

FORM.

Return of

for

from the   to the   18

	No. of Persons.	No. of Horses.	No. of Mules.	No. of Oxen.
Total				

REMARKS.

Received from at	In Figures.
Pounds of Bread	
Pounds of Meat	
Pints of Wine	
Pounds of Barley	
Pounds of Indian Corn. ...	
Pounds of Straw	
Pounds of Wood	
For which I have signed Triplicate Receipts.	

N.B. The quantities to be written in words at length, no erasure or interlineation to be allowed.

12. Lieutenant General Cotton will proceed and take the command of the troops at Merida, and will receive his instructions from the Quarter-Master General.

o 2

13. Briga-

13. Brigadier General Slade will, till further orders, command the brigade of light Cavalry hitherto under the command of Lieutenant General Cotton.

Memorandum.—Assistant Surgeon Waters, 2d battalion 7th Foot, being removed to the 1st battalion, Hospital Mate Duigenan will act as Assistant Surgeon to the 2d battalion 7th Foot till his Majesty's pleasure is known.

G. O.   ADJUTANT GENERAL'S OFFICE.
Lisbon, 11th Oct. 1809.

1. THE Commander of the Forces is apprehensive that his orders, respecting the returning of carts in the possession of the regiments of the army, have not been understood, as they have not been obeyed; he now desires, that upon the receipt of this order, the Officers commanding regiments will send to the Commissary of the brigade or division, in which the regiment is placed, all carts in possession of the regiments to which native drivers are attached.

2. In future, if any regiment should retain a cart after it shall have performed the special service for which it has been supplied to the regiment, the hire of such cart for the number of days it will be so detained will be charged against the subsistence of the regiment.

3. The Officers commanding brigades will report to the Quarter-Master General, on the 18th instant, whether this order has been obeyed.

4. The carts with oxen or mules without native drivers are to be retained in the service of the regiments which have them, and these regiments are to send to the Quar-
ter-

ter-Master General a monthly return of them on the 1st of every month.

5. The Officer commanding the Cavalry will take care that each detached squadron of the Cavalry receives and carries into execution this order.

6. The clothing and other regimental stores received by the different regiments of the army are to be delivered out to the soldiers, as soon as possible, after they shall be received, as it will be impossible to provide carriages to remove them in case any movement should be made.

7. The Officers commanding brigades will report to the Quarter-Master General that this order has been obeyed on the 5th day after each regiment shall have received clothing or stores.

ADJUTANT GENERAL's OFFICE.
Badajoz, 16th Oct. 1809.

G. O.

1. AT a General Court Martial held at Lisbon, on Saturday the 7th October, 1809, whereof Brigadier General Slade was President, and Lieutenant R. Crompton, 9th Foot, Deputy Judge Advocate, Private Charles Rankin, of the 23d Light Dragoons, was arraigned on the following charges, viz.

1st. Having, about the month of July last, stolen in the house of Marshal Beresford, at Lisbon, a silver spoon.

2d. Having, about the 26th or 27th of August last, altered a ration return from two to twelve rations, with an intention to defraud the Portuguese Commissary, or Captain Warr.

o 3

3d. Having

3d. Having, during the retreat of the British army in Spain, in the month of January last, in the town of Lugo, stolen from Lieutenant William Sewel, 16th Light Dragoons, Aide-de-Camp to Marshal Beresford, a gold watch and seals, a gold tooth-pick case, and a small silver essence box.

4th. On suspicion of having stolen a valuable snuff-box and other trinkets, as also a sum of money which he had in his possession, and is supposed to have acquired unlawfully, being unable to account for how he came by it, and endeavoured to conceal from Captain Warr, when discharged from his service, that he had such trinkets and sums of money in his possession.

The Court after duly weighing the evidence and what the prisoner, Charles Rankin, has urged in his defence, is of opinion that he is guilty of the 1st charge. The 2d charge was withdrawn by desire of the prosecutor. The Court is of opinion that Private Charles Rankin is guilty of the last part of the 3d charge, viz.

Having stolen from Lieutenant William Sewell, 16th Light Dragoons, Aide-de-Camp to Marshal Beresford, a small silver essence box: but is of opinion that the prisoner, Charles Rankin, is guilty of the 4th charge.

Upon the whole, the Court adjudge the prisoner, Charles Rankin, Private Soldier in the 23d Light Dragoons, to suffer *Death* by being hanged by the neck, at such time and place as his Excellency the Commander of the Forces may please to direct.

The Court recommends that Captain Warr will take immediate steps to find out the owners of the valuable snuff-box and other trinkets that the prisoner, Charles Rankin, had in his possession, which he acquired unlawfully;

fully; and the Court further recommends that the sums of money that were found in possession of the prisoner, amounting to 49*l*. 2*s*. 8½*d*. sterling, it being impossible for them to trace from whom the money was stolen, should be appropriated to any of the charitable funds for the relief of Soldiers' Widows, in such manner as his Excellency the Commander of the Forces may please to direct; which sentence has been confirmed by the Commander of the Forces.

The sentence of the General Court Martial on Charles Rankin is to be carried into execution in presence of the troops composing the garrison of Lisbon, at the first evening parade after the receipt of this order. The essence box and spoon stolen are to be returned to Major Sewell and Marshal Beresford respectively; and the snuff-box and other trinkets to Captain Warr, according to the sentence of the General Court Martial, by the Town Major of Lisbon. The Town Major will likewise hand over to the Commissary General the sum of 49*l*. 2*s*. 8½*d*. sterling, which sum the Commissary General will contribute to the fund, instituted at Lloyd's, for the benefit of the Widows and Children of Soldiers, as directed by the sentence of the General Court Martial.

2d. The Court, composed of another member, Major Davy Ross, of the 38th Regiment, ordered to sit in the room of Major Assler, 5th Line battalion King's German Legion, proceeded to the trial of Captain Edward Scott, of the 45th Regiment, arraigned on the following charges, viz.

1st. For most unofficer and ungentlemanlike conduct, in being concerned in an affray which took place in the city of Lisbon, on the night of the 3d of March last.

2d. For

2d. For conduct unbecoming the character of an Officer and a Gentleman, in pursuing with a drawn sword,
through the streets of Lisbon, three or four inhabitants, on
the same night, viz. the 3d of March, 1809.

The Court having weighed and considered the evidence
adduced on the part of the prosecution, and what the prisoner has urged in his defence with respect to the 1st article of charge preferred against him, is of opinion that he
was concerned in an affray which took place in the city of
Lisbon on the night of the 3d of March last, 1809, in
consequence of an attack made upon him by some Spa-
niards, in the house of Maria Da Luz; but that under
the above circumstance he was not guilty of most unofficer and ungentlemanlike conduct, and do therefore acquit him of that part of the charge.   With respect to the
2d article of charge preferred against the prisoner, Captain Edward Scott, the Court is of opinion that he is
guilty of having pursued with a drawn sword through the
streets of Lisbon three or four inhabitants on the same
night, viz. 3d of March, 1809; but in consequence of
the great provocation he had previously received, as noticed in the decision of the Court on the 1st charge, do
acquit him of a conduct unbecoming the character of an
Officer and a Gentleman; upon the whole the Court does
adjudge the prisoner, Captain Edward Scott, to be repri-
mended in such manner and at such time and place as his
Excellency the Commander of the Forces shall be pleased
to order; which sentence has been confirmed by the Commander of the Forces.

The Commander of the Forces cannot avoid to draw
the attention of the army in particular to the circumstances of Captain Scott's case, and to urge them to avoid
misfortunes

misfortunes similar to those he has met with, by avoiding the places in which they originate. The Commander of the Forces will not aggravate the distress which Captain Scott must feel, by entering into further particulars; but in pursuance of the sentence of the General Court Martial, he hereby reprimands him for his conduct, at Lisbon, on the night of the 3d March, 1809.

Adjutant General's Office.
Badajoz, 17th Oct. 1809.

G. O.

At a General Court Martial held by virtue of a warrant, and in pursuance of an order from his Excellency Lord Viscount Wellington, K. B. Badajos, 4th October, 1809, Brigadier General R. Crawford, President, Lieutenant Henry Johnson, of the 1st battalion 88th Regiment, was arraigned on the following charges, viz.

1st. For conduct unbecoming an Officer, on the 30th March last, by expressing to Major Vandileur, the Commanding Officer of his regiment, in presence of the Officers, that he did not know Major Vandileur, or acknowledge him to be Commanding Officer, at the mess of the Officers of his regiments, or words to that effect, thereby disavowing the power and authority invested in his Commanding Officer, and in violation of the orders of his Majesty to all Officers.

2d. For making use of improper and disrespectful language, in presence of the Officers of his regiment, to Major Vandileur, then Commanding Officer, whilst in the execution of his duty, on the morning of the 30th March, in breach of the Articles of War.

The

The Court having maturely considered the evidence adduced on the prosecution against the prisoner, together with what he has alleged in his defence, are of opinion he is guilty of the charges preferred against him, being in breach of the Articles of War, and do by virtue thereof sentence him, Lieutenant Johnson, of the 88th Regiment, to be suspended from rank and pay for six calendar months.

The Court are induced to award this lenient sentence, in consideration of the extremely irritating language Lieutenant Johnson had received at the meeting of the Officers of the 88th Regiment, from his then Commanding Officer, Major Vandileur, without his having in any degree whatsoever provoked him; which sentence has been confirmed by his Excellency the Commander of the Forces : the suspension of Lieutenant Johnson from rank and pay is to commence from the 14th instant inclusive.

2d. Before the same General Court Martial, on the 7th October, 1809, John Campbell and George Lee, Private Soldiers of the 2d battalion 24th Regiment, were arraigned for desertion from the said regiment, on or about the 15th September, 1809. The Court having maturely considered the evidence adduced on the prosecution against the prisoners, Private John Campbell and George Lee, together with what they have offered in their defence, are of opinion that they are both guilty of the crime laid to their charge, being in breach of the 1st article of the 6th Section of the Articles of War, and do by virtue thereof sentence them, the prisoners, John Campbell and George Lee, of the 24th Regiment, to be shot to *Death* at such time and place as his Excellency the Commander of the

Forces

Forces may deem fit; which sentence has been confirmed by the Commander of the Forces.

The sentence of the General Court Martial on the prisoners, John Campbell and George Lee, is to be carried into execution in presence of Brigadier General Cameron's brigade, at Lobon, at the first evening parade after the receipt of this order.

3d. Before the same General Court Martial, on the 10th October, Private William Harnyman, of the 1st Light Dragoons King's German Legion, was arraigned for deserting from his regiment, on or about the 22d September, 1809. The Court having maturely considered the evidence adduced on the prosecution against the prisoner, together with what he has offered in his defence, are of opinion he is guilty of the charge preferred against him, being in breach of the Articles of War, and do by virtue thereof sentence him to receive 800 Lashes, at such time and place as his Excellency the Commander of the Forces may deem fit; which sentence has been confirmed by his Excellency the Commander of the Forces.

The Commander of the Forces is induced to pardon the prisoner, Harnyman, in consequence of his good character.

The Commander of the Forces desires the Officers of the army, particularly those of the German Legion, to understand that a soldier must not be forced to become a servant, as soldiers are invited voluntarily to serve their Officers, but it must be by their own choice.

4th. Before the same General Court Martial, on the 5th October, 1809, Gunner Frederick Knaupft, 2d company Royal German Artillery, was arraigned for desertion,

on

on or about the 5th August, 1809, when on leave for one day from the camp, on the Rio del Monte de Truxillo. The Court having maturely considered the evidence adduced on the prosecution against the prisoner, together with what he has offered in his defence, are of opinion he is guilty of the charge preferred against him, being in breach of the Articles of War, and do by virtue thereof sentence him to receive 800 Lashes, in the usual manner, at such time and place as the Commander of the Forces may deem fit; which sentence has been confirmed by the Commander of the Forces.

The Commander of the Forces is induced to pardon Gunner Frederick Knaupft, at the recommendation of the General Court Martial.

5th. The General Court Martial, of which Brigadier General R. Crawford is President, is adjourned, and the Officers composing it are to return to their duty.

6th. At a General Court Martial held at Lisbon, on the 28th September, 1809, by order of his Excellency Lord Viscount Wellington, Brigadier General Slade, President, Lieutenant William Perse, of the 45th Regiment, was arraigned on the following charge, viz.

For most unofficerlike and ungentlemanlike conduct, in being concerned in an affray which took place in the city of Lisbon, on the night of the 3d of March last, 1809.

The Court having maturely considered the evidence adduced on the part of the prosecution, and what the prisoner had urged in his defence, are of opinion that he was concerned in an affray, which took place in the city of Lisbon, on the night of the 3d of March last, 1809; but no guilt attached to him, in as much as it appears he was

extremely

extremely active, and did all in his power to quell the disturbance, and do therefore acquit him; which sentence has been confirmed by the Commander of the Forces.

7th. The General Court Martial, of which Brigadier General Slade is President, is dissolved, and the members are to join their corps.

8th. Hospital Mate George Walsh, having been tried by a General Court Martial, is to be released from his close arrest, but is to continue at Lisbon in arrest at large till further orders, and is to shew himself daily at the Town Major's Office.

The Commander of the Forces is always concerned when he is obliged to place an Officer in close arrest; but if Officers break their arrest and conceal themselves, and quit the situation pointed out for their residence, they must expect that the Commander of the Forces will use the power which he has to compel them to conduct themselves as British Officers ought.

G. O.

ADJUTANT GENERAL'S OFFICE.
Badajoz, 24th Oct. 1809.

PAYMASTERS of regiments are to receive from the Deputy Paymaster General, the amount of their estimates to the 24th October, those of the 1st and 4th divisions of the army to-morrow the 25th instant; those of the 2d and 3d divisions on the 26th, and those of the cavalry on the 27th instant; estimates to the 24th November to be immediately sent in to the Deputy Paymaster General.

G. O.

ADJUTANT GENERAL's OFFICE.
Badajoz, 20th Oct. 1809.

G. O.

1. COMPLAINTS having been made of the irregularity
and difficulties which exist in quartering Officers in Lisbon, owing to the disobedience of the General Orders of
the late Commander of the Forces, of the 14th March
last, these Orders are again published, and the attention of
the Officers of the army is again called to them.

2. Officers now quartered in Lisbon are forthwith to
return to the Assistant Quarter-Master General, at Lisbon,
their names, stating where they are quartered; and the
Assistant Quarter-Master General will make out a general List of the Officers and their quarters, and will deliver
it to the Superintendant of the Police.

3. Officers who will omit to give their names and places
of abode to the Assistant Quarter-Master General, according to this order, will be considered as having quitted
the house in which they were billetted, others will be billetted on the house, and the Officer, who will be guilty
of this omission, will be obliged to hire a lodging.

4. In future all Officers moving from one place to another, in Portugal or Spain, are to have a Route from the
Quarter-Master General's department, which is to specify
where the Officer is to halt each day.

5. The Officers of the Quarter-Master General's department, who will grant these Routes upon application
for them, will keep copies of them; and the Officers, who
will receive them, will send them to the Quarter-Master
General on their arrival at their destination.

6. Officers applying for a Route to quit Lisbon are to
return their Billets to the Assistant Quarter-Master General,

ral, who will forthwith send it to the Superintendant of the Police.

GENERAL ORDERS, 14th March, 1809, alluded to in the foregoing Orders.

ADJUTANT GENERAL'S OFFICE.

G. O.   *Lisbon, 14th March,* 1809.

REPRESENTATIONS having been made to the Commander of the Forces on the subject of the inconvenience sustained, both by the inhabitants and Officers of the army, from want of better arrangements regarding billets, His Excellency finds it necessary to establish the following regulations.

1. All General Officers and Heads of Departments will apply, and receive their billets, from the Deputy Quarter-Master General.

2. All other Officers are to receive their billets from the Town Major.

3. No Officer quitting Lisbon is to retain his quarters, but he must give back his billet to the department from which he has received it, whether the Deputy Quarter-Master General, or Town Major.

4. No Officer is on any account to select any particular house, nor to choose his own quarters; all that they can expect is, that each shall be provided with a quarter suitable to his rank.

5. Colonels will be entitled to four rooms, Field Officers three, Captains two, Subalterns one room for each. Staff Officers will have quarters allotted them according to their comparative rank they hold in their several departments, civil or military.

6. No

6. No Officer, under the rank of a General Officer, is to require more than two servants beds at the most.

7. No Officer is on any account to deliver over his billet to another.

8. No billet is to be exchanged for any Officer of any rank, without previous application to the Deputy Quarter-Master General. If the Officer applying be under the rank of a General Officer, he is to apply through the Town Major, who will presently explain to the Deputy Quarter-Master General the cause of the application.

9. No Officer whatever has any pretensions to look for or require any thing more than his lodgings, where he is billeted.

10. The Town Major, in applying to the Intendant General for billets, is to specify the several ranks for which they are required, and if they are for Staff Officers, he will indicate the comparative rank held by them.

All Officers whatever who have got into houses without regular billets, are to send in their names to the Deputy Quarter-Master General, that billets may be either made out for the present quarters they now occupy, or other quarters allotted to them.

(A True Copy)

(Signed)   A. WALSH.

Lieut. Col. Town Major.

ADJUTANT GENERAL's OFFICE.

Badajoz, 28th *Oct.* 1809.

G. O.

Memorandum—L. Donovan, Esq. is appointed Deputy Commissary General, with the army serving in Spain and Portugal.

G. O.

ADJUTANT GENERAL'S OFFICE.

G. O. *Badajoz, 30th Oct.* 1809.

1. A CERTAIN number of blankets having arrived, they are for the present to be issued to the Infantry at the rate of one for two men; the Commanding Officers of regiments will make requisitions accordingly, upon the Quarter-Master General for them, and the Quarter-Master General will take measures for issuing the blankets without loss of time to the troops at the several stations.

2. These blankets are to be considered as articles of regimental necessaries, and are to be carried by the men to whom they are delivered, who are to be accountable for them, and to produce them at every weekly inspection of necessaries; as soon as a large quantity of them shall arrive from Lisbon, a sufficient number will be issued for one blanket to each soldier.

3. The General Court Martial, of which Brigadier General R. Crawford is President, is dissolved.

> ERRATUM *in the General Orders (17th Oct. No.7)*— For the word " *dissolved*" read " *adjourned till further orders,*" and the members are to join their corps.

4. An arrangement has been made to dispatch a packet from Lisbon to England every Sunday, and the packet will be made up at Head-Quarters for England, and will be sent to Lisbon on every Thursday.

5. A General Court Martial will assemble at Montigo, on Wednesday the 1st November, for the trial of such prisoners as may be brought before it.

DETAIL.

Lieutenant General Hill, President.

	Field Officers.	Captains.	Subalterns.
2d Division	2 —	5 —	7

Members' names, rank, and dates of commissions will be sent to the Assistant Adjutant General of the 2d division without loss of time.

G. O.

ADJUTANT GENERAL'S OFFICE.
Badajoz, 31st Oct. 1809.

1. ORDERS having been received to draft the horses of the 23d Light Dragoons, they are to be distributed to the other regiments of Light Dragoons, in the following proportions, viz.

	Horses.
1st Hussars	58
14th Light Dragoons	126
16th do. do.	81
3d Dragoon Guards } 4th Dragoons	18
Total	283

The collars and chains will be delivered over with the horses to the regiments which receive them; the forge carts are to be delivered over to such of the regiments as Lieutenant General Payne will think require them. Lieutenant General Payne will also arrange the mode in which

the

the horses shall be selected by the different regiments, and he will order sufficient numbers of men from each to Villa Vicoza, to receive charge of the horses allotted to them. Lieutenant General Payne will order the Commanding Officer of the 23d Dragoons, to transfer to the regiments respectively, into which the horses will be drafted, such number of swords, pistols, carbines, sets of horse-appointments, corn sacks, water decks, and blankets, as will complete the effective strength of those regiments with the articles of equipment which they require, and he will make a return to the Adjutant General, of the articles allotted to each regiment under this order.

The Commanding Officers of the regiments of Dragoons to which these articles will be transferred, are to give receipts for them. Lieutenant General Payne will order a Board to assemble to value the different articles, whether belonging to the Dragoons or to the Colonel, which will be transferred under this order, a copy of whose proceedings are to be sent to the Adjutant General, and copies will be sent by him to each of the regiments concerned; the Board will report the proportional value of each article upon the following principle, and they are to be paid for accordingly by the Colonel of the regiments to which the articles will have been transferred.

Full Value, or Prime Cost.

Three Quarters	$\frac{3}{4}$	of P. C.
One Half	$\frac{1}{2}$	P. C.
One Third	$\frac{1}{3}$	P. C.
One Fourth	$\frac{1}{4}$	P. C.

The Board will specify in their report the regiment to which each article has been transferred. As soon as the

horses

horses shall be drafted, the 23d Dragoons are to march to Lisbon, for which purpose, the Quarter-Master General will send a route to Lieutenant General Payne ; the Lieutenant General will order at the same time, such men of the other regiments of cavalry as belong to the recruiting troops to march to Lisbon, where arrangements will be made to embark the whole for England.

The Commander of the Forces cannot allow the 23d regiment of Light Dragoons to quit the army without expressing his concern upon losing their services; the severe loss, however, which they sustained in a most gallant and effectual charge in the battle of Talavera, has rendered it desirable that they should have an opportunity to recruit; and the Commander of the Forces hopes, that before much time will elapse, they will be in full strength, and will have fresh opportunities of distinguishing themselves.

2. The Cavalry are to be brigaded as follows, viz.

3d Dragoon Guards . . . . . .
4th Dragoons . . . . } Brig. Gen. Fane

1st Hussars . . . .
16th Light Dragoons . . . . . . } Brig. Gen. Anson

1st or Royal Regt. of Dragoons .
14th Light Dragoons . . . . . } Brig. Gen. Slade

3. The Veterinary Surgeons and Farriers of the Royals are to be entitled, from the date of their landing, to the allowances granted Veterinary Surgeons and Farriers by the General Orders of the 15th July, No. 1.

G. A. O.

ADJUTANT GENERAL's OFFICE.

G. A. O. *Badajoz, 31st Oct.* 1809.

1. CAPTAIN the Marquis of Tweedale is to act as Deputy Assistant Quarter-Master General until his Majesty's pleasure is known.

2. Captain Kelly, of the Royal Dragoons, is to act as Deputy Assistant Quarter-Master General, until his Majesty's pleasure is known.

3. The Commander of the Forces requests the Officers commanding divisions will make their divisions march a distance of not less than three leagues in marching order twice a week, besides the formations which the nature of the ground may induce them to make in the course of the march. The Officers commanding the cavalry and artillery will also, by frequent exercise, prevent the horses of losing the habit of marching.

4. Major General the Hon. G. Lowrey Cole is appointed to command the brigade of Infantry, hitherto under the command of Brigadier General Campbell, during the absence of the latter.

5. The Commander of the Forces desires that the Officers commanding brigades of artillery will distinctly understand, that he holds them responsible for the condition of the artillery horses attached to their brigades, and they will take measures that the Officers and men of the gunner drivers do their duty by taking proper care of them.

ADJUTANT GENERAL'S OFFICE.

G. O. *Badajoz, 26th Oct.* 1809.

1. BREVET Major Murphy, of the 88th regiment, is appointed to command and take charge of the detachments

 of

of sick convalescents on command, &c. of the regiments of the army which are at Lisbon and Belem, from the 25th instant.

Colonel Walsh will make over to him all accounts, papers, &c.

2. Brevet Major Geddes, of the 83d regiment, is appointed Town Major of Lisbon from the 25th instant.

ADJUTANT GENERAL's OFFICE.
G. O.   *Badajoz, 1st Nov.* 1809.

THE five companies of the 60th regiment attached to Colonel Donkin's brigade, will march from Campo Mayor on the 2d instant; and the 40th regiment from Badajoz on the 3d instant, according to routes they will receive from the Quarter-Master General.

ADJUTANT GENERAL's OFFICE.
G. O.   *Badajoz, 2d Nov.* 1809.

A PROPORTION of orderly men, and Non-commissioned Officers, *one* to *ten* of the former, and *one* to thirty of the latter, to be sent with the sick from the 2d division to the hospital at Estremoz.

ADJUTANT GENERAL's CFFICE.
G. O.   *Badajoz, 3d Nov.* 1809.

Memorandum—Captain Alexander de Roverea, of the Sicilian regiment, is appointed Aide-de-Camp to Major General the Hon. G. L. Cole.

G. O.

ADJUTANT GENERAL'S OFFICE.
Badajoz, 13th Nov. 1809.

G. O.

1. THE men of the following corps are to be charged six-pence per diem, for their rations, from the 29th August, viz. 14th and 16th Light Dragoons, and 3d division of Infantry.

3. *Copy of a letter from the Commander in Chief, to Lieutenant General Lord Viscount Wellington, dated,*

HORSE GUARDS,
5th Oct. 1809.

MY LORD,

HAVING laid before the King the proceedings of a General Court Martial held at Jaracejo, on the 18th of August, and at Merida on the 27th and 28th of the same month, for the trial of Lieutenant Ludlow, of the 2d battalion 48th regiment, who was arraigned upon the undermentioned charges, viz.

1st, For being drunk on the march of the regiment from Castello Branco on the 2d July.

2d, For using highly improper language towards Ensign Pardy, during the march from Castello Branco on the same day; upon which charges, the Court came to the following decision.

The Court having maturely considered the evidence adduced on the prosecution in support of the charges against the prisoner Lieutenant Ludlow, together with what he has offered in his defence, are of opinion that he is guilty of the first charge preferred against him, viz. for being

P 4

drunk

drunk on the march of the regiment from Castello Branco, on the 2d July; being a breach of the 9th article, 14th section, of the Articles of War; and do by virtue thereof, sentence him, Lieutenant Ludlow, to be cashiered. The Court are further of opinion that the prisoner Lieutenant Ludlow is not guilty of the 2d charge preferred against him, viz. for using highly improper language towards Ensign Pardy, during the march from Castello Branco on the same day; and do therefore acquit him of the same.

I have to acquaint your Lordship, that his Majesty has been pleased to approve of the findings and sentence of the Court. Your Lordship will therefore acquaint me with the day upon which the sentence is made known to the prisoner Lieutenant Ludlow, as from that day he will cease to receive pay in his Majesty's service.

(Signed)   D. DUNDAS.

4. *Copy of a Letter from the Commander in Chief, to Lieutenant General Lord Viscount Wellington, dated,*

HORSE GUARDS.
5th Oct. 1809.

My Lord,

HAVING laid before the King the proceedings of a General Court Martial held at Merida, on the 31st August, 1809, for the trial of Isaac Buxton, Paymaster, 2d battalion 24th regiment, who was arraigned on the undermentioned charge, viz.

For absenting himself from his regiment without leave at or near Talavera, on or about the 3d August, 1809, and proceeding to the rear without leave, thereby acting highly prejudicial to good order and military discipline.

Upon

Upon which the Court came to the following decision. The Court having maturely weighed and considered the evidence produced on the prosecution against the prisoner Isaac Buxton, Esq. Paymaster, 2d battalion 24th regiment, together with what he has offered in his defence, are of opinion he is guilty of the charge preferred against him, being in breach of the Articles of War; and do by virtue thereof, sentence him, the prisoner Isaac Buxton, Esq. Paymaster, 2d battalion 24th regiment, to be cashiered.

I have to acquaint your Lordship, that his Majesty was pleased to approve and confirm the sentence of the Court; but taking into consideration all the circumstances of the case as they appear upon the face of the proceedings, and as recommended by the Court as well as by your Lordship, his Majesty was pleased to extend to the prisoner his most gracious pardon; and to command that he should be restored to the functions of his commission.

(Signed)   D. DUNDAS.
Commander in Chief.

5. The General Court Martial of which Major General Tilson was President, is dissolved.

6. A General Court Martial will assemble at Badajoz, on the 15th instant, at 11 o'clock, for the trial of such prisoners as may be brought before it.

Major General the Hon. G. L. Cole to be President.

	Field Officers.	Captains.	Subalterns.
Artillery	0	1	0
Divisions of Cavalry	1	1	0
1st Division of Infantry	1	2	1
3d ditto	1	2	0
4th ditto	1	2	1
Total . .	4	8	2

Members

Members names and dates of Commissions and lists of evidences, to be sent in to the Adjutant General's Office, by to-morrow at orderly hour, directed to the Deputy Judge Advocate; evidences to be warned and to attend.

ADJUTANT GENERAL'S OFFICE.
Badajoz, 14th Nov. 1809.

G. O.

1. AT a General Court Martial, held by virtue of a warrant in pursuance of an order from his Excellency Lord Viscount Wellington, at Montego, the 1st of November, 1809, and of which Lieutenant General Hill was President:

Thomas Jones, private in the 1st battalion 3d regiment, or Buffs, arraigned for desertion from his regiment, on or about the 9th April, 1809.

The Court having maturely and deliberately weighed and considered the evidences adduced on the prosecution against the prisoner, private Thomas Jones, of the 3d regiment or Buffs, together with what he has offered in his defence, are of opinion, he is guilty of the charge preferred against him, being a breach of the 1st article 6th section of the Articles of War; and by virtue thereof, do sentence him, the prisoner, private Thomas Jones, of the 3d regiment or Buffs, to be shot to death, at such time and place, as his Excellency the Commander of the Forces may deem fit: which sentence has been confirmed by his Excellency the Commander of the Forces.

The sentence of the General Court Martial on Thomas Jones, private soldier in the 3d regiment or Buffs, is to be carried into execution by a detachment of the Buffs, under

the

the direction of the Assistant Provost Marshal, of the 2d division of Infantry, on the afternoon of the 14th instant, in presence of that part of Lieutenant General Hill's division stationed at Montego.

2. Before the same General Court Martial, Edward Bayley, of the 1st battalion 48th regiment, was arraigned for murder, in wounding private John Howe, of the same regiment, in the groin, with an iron rod or instrument, on or about the 6th October, 1809; and of which wound, or wounds, the said John Howe, private in the 1st battalion 48th regiment, did die, on or about the 16th of the same month.

The Court having maturely and deliberately weighed and considered the evidences adduced on the prosecution against the prisoner, private Edward Bayley, of the 1st battalion 48th regiment, together with what he has offered in his defence, and the evidence thereon, are of opinion he is not guilty of the charge preferred against him, and do therefore acquit him of the same : which sentence has been confirmed by his Excellency the Commander of the Forces.

3. The General Court Martial of which Lieutenant General Hill is President, is dissolved.

5. The Commander of the Forces requests the General Officers will discontinue the marching exercise, ordered by the General Orders of the 31st October, No. 3, while the roads shall be injured by the fall of rain.

G. O.

ADJUTANT GENERAL'S OFFICE.
Badajoz, 15th Nov. 1809.

COLONEL the Hon. Edward Pakenham, is appointed to act as an Assistant in the Adjutant General's department.

Captain

Captain the Hon. E. Charles Cocks, of 16th Light Dragoons, is appointed Aide-de-Camp to Lieutenant General Sir Stapleton Cotton, from the 31st August last.

G. O. ADJUTANT GENERAL's OFFICE.
Badajoz, 16th Nov. 1809.

1. CAPTAIN Gore, of the 9th Dragoons, is appointed an extra Aide-de-Camp to General Beresford.

2. A General Court Martial, consisting of a President and 14 members, to assemble at Lisbon, on Monday the 20th of November, for the trial of such prisoners as may be brought before them.

Colonel Peacocke, President.

The detail of members to be furnished at Lisbon.

3. The Officers commanding regiments of cavalry are requested to carry into execution, as soon as it may be convenient to them, the directions contained in the following letter from the War Office, of the 14th September, 1809, and the Quarter-Masters who will retire under the directions of this letter, are to be ordered to proceed to Lisbon, from whence they will go to England with the 23d Dragoons.

(CIRCULAR.) WAR-OFFICE.
14th Sept. 1809.

SIR,

4. I HAVE the honour to acquaint you, his Majesty has been pleased to approve of an arrangement for abolishing gradually, the situations of troop Quarter-Masters in the cavalry, and providing for the performance of the
duties

duties hitherto attached to that situation, by the appointment of Troop Serjeant Majors.

Such of the present Troop Quarter-Masters in the regiments of cavalry as are unfit for further service, are accordingly to be allowed to retire on a provision for life; which provision, if they have served 40 years, at the time of their retirement, is to be equal to their full pay, viz. 5s. 6d. per day; if otherwise, 3s. per day.

Returns of the Troop Quarter-Masters so entitled to retire, are to be transmitted to the Commander in Chief.

These retired allowances will be borne on the half-pay establishment as military allowances, and issued half-yearly under the same regulations as half-pay.

To each troop in which the appointment of Quarter-Masters shall cease in consequence of the above arrangement, a Troop Serjeant Major is to be appointed, with the pay of 3s. per day, exclusive of the allowances for his horse.

As a part of the present arrangement, the pay of the regimental Serjeant Majors is to be increased to 3s. 6d. a day, exclusive of the allowances for his horse, and the said increase will be allowed to be charged from the 25th June last inclusive.

A Regimental Quarter-Master will also be added to the establishment of each regiment of cavalry, with pay to commence from the date of his commission, at the rate of 8s. a day, including the allowance of 2s. a day for his horse.———I have the honour to be, Sir,

Your most obedient humble servant,

(Signed)   J. W. GORDON.

To Major General Payne, }
  of the 23d Lt. Dragoons. }

6. The

6. The Commanding Officers of such regiments as have with them more clothing than they require for their men, are to apply to the Commissary General for carts to remove it to Lisbon. He will supply carts for that purpose.

The carts will proceed according to a route from the Quarter-Master General, under escorts to be supplied by the regiments to which the clothing belongs.

7. An additional supply of blankets having arrived, the Officers commanding regiments of Infantry of the army, are to make a requisition for one for every fourth man of the Non-commissioned Officers and soldiers under their command respectively; this supply will complete three-fourths of the number of each regiment of Infantry.

8. The Commander of the Forces requests the Officers commanding regiments will take care that the Officers who have lately joined this army, are made acquainted with all the General Orders which have at different times been given out.

ADJUTANT GENERAL'S OFFICE.
G. A. O.   *Badajoz, 17th Nov.* 1809.

1. THE Paymaster General is to advance to the Officers of the 2d battalion 61st regiment, one month's subsistence to the 24th of December, upon an estimate transmitted to him by Major Godfrey.

ADJUTANT GENERAL'S OFFICE.
G. A. O.   *Badajoz, 19th Nov.* 1809.

MR. Showman is appointed an acting Assistant Commissary till his Majesty's pleasure is known.

Mr.

Mr. St. Remy is appointed an acting Assistant Commissary till his Majesty's pleasure is known.

Captain William Campbell, of the 23d or Welsh Fusileers, is appointed to act as a Deputy Assistant in the Quarter-Master General's department, till his Majesty's pleasure is known. Captain W. Campbell is attached to the 3d division of Infantry.

Major Smyth, of the 2d battalion 45th regiment, will remain till further orders with the 1st battalion.

G. O.

ADJUTANT GENERAL'S OFFICE.
Badajoz, 20th Nov. 1809.

1. The sick are to be removed from the regimental hospitals at Badajoz, Talavera, Lobon, and Montigo, as soon as possible, according to the plan; the details of which are in the possession of the Inspector of hospitals.

The Officers commanding regiments will be so good to attend to the directions of the Inspector of hospitals respecting this removal. Great care must be taken that the men to be removed are sent at an early hour, so that they may arrive at their destination before the close of the day.

The Officers commanding at the several stations will take care that the proportion of Officers and Non-commissioned Officers, according to the General Order 13th June, No. 4, are sent with each detachment of sick.

G. O.

ADJUTANT GENERAL'S OFFICE.
Badajoz, 21st Nov. 1809.

G. O.

(Copy)

HORSE GUARDS.
15th June, 1809.

SIR,

THE subject of the loss in camp equipage issued to the troops on foreign service, having been brought under the consideration of Government, I think it necessary to transmit to you the enclosed memorandum, containing a regulation on this head, with a scale of the full and half value of the articles of camp equipage; and to desire that the same may be observed by the troops under your command in all cases where it may apply.

I have the honour to be, SIR, &c. &c.

(Signed)   D. DUNDAS.
Commander in Chief.

To Lieutenant General Sir
A. Wellesley, K. B.

HORSE GUARDS.
30th May, 1809.

Memorandum—The subject of the loss in camp equipage issued to the troops on foreign service, having been brought under the consideration of Government, the Commander in Chief is pleased to direct that the following regulations should be adopted, founded upon the suggestion of the Comptrollers of army accompts, as transmitted by the Secretary at War, in a letter to the Quarter-Master General, dated 17th May, 1809.

General Officers commanding on foreign stations are to make it known to the different corps under their command,

mand, that they will be called upon to pay for such articles of camp equipage and camp. necessaries which, being in charge of the corps respectively, are lost through neglect, or destroyed from wilful abuse, at a rate founded on the value of the same, as stated in the accompanying schedule: with a view to this regulation being carried into effect, the principal Officers of Commissariat upon foreign stations will be furnished with similar schedules of the full and half value of camp equipage, in order that such articles may be charged against the corps, with reference to the existing state of the different articles at the time of their being so lost or destroyed. The fact of the loss or destruction of camp equipage to be ascertained by a competent Board, assembled under the orders of the General in command, whose decision having been approved, is to be transmitted to the senior Officer of the Commissariat by the Quarter-Master General's department of the army.

When blankets or bedding are issued for the use of invalids, or women, at the time of their embarking to return home from a foreign station, the Officer, or Non-commissioned Officer in charge of the detachment, is to give a receipt of the stores issued to the detachment from under whose charge they were given out; and it is to be the duty of such Officers or Non-commissioned Officers to cause the said articles to be collected, previous to the disembarkation of the detachment, and to deliver them to the Master of the Transport, taking his receipt for the same.

Upon landing, the Officer or Non-commissioned Officer is to transmit a copy of the receipt so taken to the Commissioners of Transports, London, in order that the

Master may be held accountable for the delivery of the articles given into his charge.

The Officer or Non-commissioned Officer is further to transmit a copy of the Master's receipt for the stores given over to him to the Store-keeper General, under cover to the Secretary at War, London; to which a copy of the receipt is to be annexed; a return of the articles originally delivered out to the detachment, with an account of any deficiency which may have arisen during the passage, assigning the cause for the same.

Scale of Return of full and half Value of Articles of Camp Equipage, 13th December, 1806.

	Full Value.			Half Value.		
	£.	s.	d.	£.	s.	d.
Round tent, Duke of York's pattern, with Poles, Pins, Mallets, &c. complete.	5	13	0	—2	16	6
Poles per sett	0	5	6	—0	2	9
Pins large per hundred	0	6	0	—0	3	0
Do. small per hundred	0	3	6	—0	1	9
Mallets large per dozen	0	9	6	—0	4	9
Do. small per dozen	0	5	6	—0	2	9
Iron Collars each	0	1	6	—0	0	9
Camp Colour Pole	0	3	$4\frac{1}{2}$	—0	1	8
Camp Colour Flag	0	1	1	—0	0	$6\frac{1}{2}$
Powder Bag	0	8	4	—0	4	2
Drum Case	0	6	$1\frac{1}{4}$	—0	3	$0\frac{1}{2}$
Bill-hook	0	1	$11\frac{1}{4}$	—0	0	$11\frac{1}{2}$
Flanders Kettles	0	10	$6\frac{1}{2}$	—0	5	$3\frac{1}{4}$
Wood Canteen	0	1	$9\frac{1}{4}$	—0	0	$10\frac{1}{4}$

Wood

	Full Value.			Half Value.		
	£.	s.	d.	£.	s.	d.
Wood Canteen Strap	0	1	4	—0	0	8
Havresack	0	1	4¾	—0	0	8¼
Felling Axe	0	3	3	—0	1	7½
Cap and Sling for do.	0	2	9½	—0	1	4½
Corn Sack	0	4	0¾	—0	2	0¼
Sett of Forage Cords (4)	0	3	3	—0	1	0¼
Water Bucket	0	5	10	—0	2	11
Saddle Water Deck	0	7	6½	—0	3	9¼
Picket Rope	0	8	0½	—0	4	0¼
Do. Pole	0	3	10¼	—0	1	11
Do. Mallet	0	1	7½	—0	0	9¾
Nose-bag	0	2	4¼	—0	1	2
Pack Saddle with Trees and hanchams	4	0	2	—2	0	1
Pack Saddle with Trees & Baggage straps	3	6	8¼	—1	13	4
Paillasse	0	4	10¾	—0	2	5¼
Bolster Case	0	1	1¼	—0	0	6¾
Sheet	0	6	10½	—0	3	5¼
Blanket	0	8	11	—0	4	5½
Coverlet	0	6	0	—0	3	0¼
Hospital Marquee & Tent complete	45	10	10	–22	15	5
Ammunition Bag	0	18	0¼	—0	9	0
Medicine Panniers	1	7	7	—0	13	9½
Bridle for Bât Horse	0	11	8	—0	5	10

Captain Dance, of the 23d Light Dragoons, is appointed to act as Brigade Major to the brigade under the command of Major General Slade, until his Majesty's pleasure is known.

G. O.

ADJUTANT GENERAL'S OFFICE.

G. O.   *Badajoz, 26th Nov.* 1809.

THE General Court Martial of which Major General Cole is President, will reassemble to-morrow morning at 11 o'clock.

—————————————

ADJUTANT GENERAL'S OFFICE.

G. O.   *Badajoz, 27th Nov.* 1809.

PROCEEDINGS of a General Court Martial, Badajoz, 18th Nov. 1809.—The Court met this day for the trial of private Francis Johnstone, 1st battalion 88th regiment; but the prisoner not attending, the Court was adjourned till Monday, Nov. 20th.

Nov. 20th 1809.—The Court met this day pursuant to adjournment, and proceeded to the trial of private Francis Johnstone, 88th regiment, arraigned for desertion, on or about the 2d May, 1809, to which charge the prisoner pleaded not guilty. The Court having maturely and deliberately weighed and considered the evidence adduced on the prosecution against the prisoner, private Francis Johnstone, 88th regiment, together with what he has offered in his defence, and the prosecutor's reply, and the evidence thereon, are of opinion he is guilty of the charge preferred against him, being a breach of the Articles of War; and do by virtue thereof, sentence him, the prisoner private Francis Johnstone, 1st battalion 88th regiment, to be hung by the neck until he is dead; at such time and place as his Excellency the Commander of the Forces may deem fit—

Which

Which sentence has been confirmed by his Excellency the Commander of the Forces.

The sentence of the Court Martial on Francis Johnstone, private 88th regiment, is to be carried into execution on the evening of the 28th instant, at Campo Mayor, by the Assistant Provost Marshal at that quarter, in presence of the troops drawn out for that purpose, under the direction of the Officer commanding the 3d division of Infantry.

2. The Court met this day, and proceeded on the trial of private Nicholas Roseberry, of the 1st light battalion King's German Legion, arraigned for desertion, on or about the 29th October, 1809, to which charge the prisoner pleaded not guilty.

The Court having maturely weighed and considered the evidence adduced on the prosecution against the prisoner private Nicholas Roseberry, 1st battalion King's German Legion, together with what he has offered in his defence, are of opinion he is guilty of the charge preferred against him, being a breach of the Articles of War; and do by virtue thereof, sentence him, private Nicholas Roseberry, to receive a punishment of one thousand lashes, at such time and place as his Excellency the Commander of the Forces may deem fit—

Which sentence his Excellency the Commander of the Forces has been pleased to confirm.

The sentence of the General Court Martial on Nicholas Roseberry is to be carried into execution, by the Assistant Provost Marshal attached to the 1st division of Infantry, in presence of the troops at Talavera la Real, drawn out for that purpose, under the direction of the Officer com-

manding

manding the brigade consisting of the King's German Legion, in the afternoon of the 28th instant.

3. The Paymasters of regiments in the 1st and 3d divisions, are to receive the balances on their estimates, to the 24th December, on this day and to-morrow the 28th instant; those of the 2d and 4th divisions on the 29th and 30th; and of the cavalry on the 1st of December.

ADJUTANT GENERAL'S OFFICE.
Badajoz, 28th Nov. 1809.

G. O.

2. CAPTAIN Wells, 43d regiment, is to act as Secretary to the Board appointed to enquire into claims, and is to receive the pay of a Deputy Assistant Adjutant General for doing this duty, from the 7th October, 1809, date of the assembly of the Board, until further orders.

3. The ration of the horses of the 3d Dragoon Guards, and 4th Dragoons, is to be 12lbs. of barley, until further orders.

ADJUTANT GENERAL'S OFFICE.
Badajoz, 28th Nov. 1809.

G. A. O.

THE Paymasters of regiments having omitted to give in their estimates to the 24th December, that part of the order of the 27th instant which directs that the subsistence of the troops to that period should be advanced, is suspended; and the Paymasters of regiments are to receive only the balance of their estimates the 24th November.

The estimates to the 24th December are to be given in immediately, when the balances due upon them will be advanced;

vanced; and in future, the estimates for the subsistence of the troops are to be sent in to the Deputy Paymaster General, on the day fixed by his Majesty's regulations.

ADJUTANT GENERAL'S OFFICE.

G. O. *Badajoz, 29th Nov.* 1809.

1. As some doubts have been entertained respecting the order of the late Commander of the Forces of the 16th March, respecting the hire of native servants instead of bât men from the ranks; it is published again for general information.

2. Extracts from the General Orders by Lieutenant General Sir John Craddock, K. B. dated 16th March, 1809.

The Commander of the Forces being desirous of rendering the army in the field as effective as possible, directs that no soldier whatever acting as a servant to an Officer, shall appear in any other dress than his uniform; and on a march he is to carry his arms and accoutrements.

The servants of regimental Officers to be in the ranks on the march, and the Commander of the Forces calls on the General and other Officers in command, strictly to enforce this order.

With a view to diminish as much as possible requisitions on regiments for soldiers as servants, Lieutenant General Sir J. Craddock authorises any Officer who is entitled by the usage of the service to appear mounted, and keep a horse, to hire a servant as bât man, in lieu of a soldier, for which he will be allowed at the rate of 1 dollar per week, and a ration; but it is to be distinctly understood that this allowance is not to be extended to any persons attach-

Q 4
ed

ed to this army, who by the custom of the service are not usually entitled to soldiers to wait on them ; and whenever it is drawn, an effective soldier is to be thereby restored to the army.

. The following will be the scale for the number allowed to each rank.

	Number of bàt men or servants each.
Commander of the Forces	4
Lieutenant General	3
Major and Brigadier Generals, and Heads of Departments	2
All other Officers, Regimental and Staff	1

These men will be paid by the Deputy Commissary General monthly, on regular pay-lists being transmitted every 25th, certified by the Paymasters of corps and approved by Commanding Officers of battalions.

The returns for the General Staff Officers to be made out by departments, and to be certified by the heads of each. Those of General Officers and their families to be certified by the General Officers: a form may be had of the Deputy Commissary General.

The Commander of the Forces most strongly recommends it to all the General Officers of the army, to return immediately any bàt men they may have to their corps, and to direct their Staff to do the same ; at all events, no Officer of any rank is to employ more than one soldier of this army to attend upon him, whether he acts as his personal servant or bàt man.

3. The

3. The Officers of the army will observe that the intention of this order was, to allow the hire of a native servant instead of a bât man, or servant from the ranks, to the Officers entitled, by the custom of the service, to have bât men and servants from the ranks.

4. Field Officers of regiments are entitled each to a servant and bât man; and of course to draw the allowance for each, if they should not have the service of them.

5. The Captains each a servant, and a bât man for their company. Subaltern Officers, Adjutant, Quarter-Master, Paymaster, Surgeon, and Assistant Surgeon, each a servant; and the Surgeon a bât man for the medicine chest mule; the Paymaster one, for the mule to carry his books, and the Quarter-Master one for the mule carrying the intrenching tools.

6. The General and other Officers on the Staff who have not bât men from the regiments, are to draw the allowances allotted to each.

7. It has never been the custom of the service to allow soldiers from the ranks to attend upon the Officers of the Commissariat, or the Medical Staff; and the orders of the 16th March can not be considered as relating to them.

8. The Commander of the Forces requests that particular attention may be paid to the form of the account which must be sent in, claiming payment for these bât men, and that the General Officers, Heads of Departments, and Commanding Officers of regiments, who are to certify these bills, will not certify them for any Officer who has a servant from the ranks to attend upon him.

9. The allowance of wood for the troops in camp or cantonments is to be as follows.

Daily

Daily to each Non-commissioned Officer and private soldier . . . . } 3lbs.

—— to each Subaltern and Regimental Staff .12

—— to each Captain 21

—— to each Field Officer 30

. The Officers upon the Staff are to draw according to their rank in the army. The Officers of the Commissariat and Medical Staff are to draw each the proportion of wood, allotted to the Officer of corresponding rank in the army.

As the General Officers have Staff, &c. attached to them, their allowance of wood is unlimited; but as the supply of wood in this country is very small, and it is very difficult to be procured, the Commander of the Forces requests the General Officers of the army will observe the utmost economy in the expenditure of wood, and that they will take measures that the quantities of that article supplied for their use, are applied solely for that purpose, and not stolen or applied to the use of the owner of the house in which they are quartered. .

10. Colonel M'Kinnon, Coldstream Guards, is appointed a Colonel on the Staff until his Majesty's pleasure is known; and is to command the brigade of Infantry hitherto under the command of Colonel Donkin.

Memorandum—The following notification of promotion in the Staff of the army serving under his Excellency Lieutenant General Lord Viscount Wellington has been received.

Brigadier General John Slade, Colonel 1st Royal Dragoons, to be Major General, bearing date 24th October, 1809.

G. A. O

ADJUTANT GENERAL'S OFFICE.
Badajoz, 29th Nov. 1809.

G. A. O.

1. OFFICERS commanding brigades of Artillery are requested to give directions, that when the horses attached to their guns are sent to water, or to exercise, they may be marched regularly under the command of an Officer of the gunner drivers; an Officer of the gunner drivers should likewise attend all horse parades.

2. The Commander of the Forces requests the Officers commanding regiments to explain to both Officers and soldiers of the battalions under their command, that it is equally criminal to resist a Spanish or Portuguese sentry or guard, as it is to resist either belonging to the British army.

A guard or sentry must be understood at all times to be charged with the execution of the orders of a competent authority at the place in which either may be stationed, or may be found, and must not be resisted on any account.

Guards or sentries may mistake their orders, or may execute them improperly, and in these cases complaints must be made; but on no account must they be resisted.

ADJUTANT GENERAL'S OFFICE.
Badajoz, 1st Dec. 1809.

G. O.

1. AT a General Court Martial, held by virtue of a warrant, and in pursuance of an order from his Excellency the Rt. Hon. Lord Viscount Wellington, whereof Major General the Hon. G. Lowry Cole was President:

Lieutenant

Lieutenant Frederick Statz, 5th battalion 60th regiment, was arraigned upon the following charges.

Charge 1st, For scandalous and infamous conduct highly unbecoming the character of an Officer and a gentleman, in striking Lieutenant de Eberstein, of the same corps on the 23d Oct. 1809.

Charge 2d, For absenting himself without leave from his regiment, during the whole of the action on the 28th July, 1809. To which charges the prisoner pleaded not guilty.

OPINION.

THE Court having maturely and deliberately weighed and considered the evidence adduced on the prosecution against the prisoner Lieutenant Frederick Statz, 5th battalion 60th regiment, together what he has alleged in his defence, and the evidences thereon, are of opinion that he is not guilty of the 1st charge preferred against him, viz. of scandalous and infamous conduct, highly unbecoming the character of an Officer and a gentleman, in striking Lieutenant de Eberstein of the same corps, on the 23d Oct. 1809, from the extreme provocation the prisoner Lieutenant Statz appears to have received from Lieutenant de Eberstein; and do therefore acquit him thereof.

The Court are further of opinion, that although it appears that Lieutenant Statz was absent from his regiment on the 28th July, 1809, he has adduced sufficient evidences to justify his absence on that day, and the Court do therefore acquit him, the prisoner Lieutenant Frederick Statz, of the 2d charge preferred against him; which decision has been confirmed by his Excellency the Commander of the Forces.

2. The

2. The General Court Martial, of which Major General the Hon. Lowry Cole is President, is dissolved, and the members are to join their regiments.

3. A General Court Martial will assemble at Badajoz on Monday, 4th Dec. at 11 o'clock, for the trial of such prisoners as may be brought before it.

Brigadier General Cameron President.

DETAIL.

	Field Officers.		Captains.		Subalterns.
1st Division of Infantry . . .	2	—	1	—	1
2d do.	2	—	2	—	0
3d do.	1	—	1	—	1
4th do.	1	—	2	—	0
Total	6	—	6	—	2

Names and dates of commissions of the members, and the list of evidences to be sent in by the 3d instant at or-- derly hour, to the Adjutant General's Office, directed to the Deputy Judge Advocate.

G. O.

ADJUTANT GENERAL'S OFFICE.
Badajoz, 2d Dec. 1809.

1. The order of the 29th ult. relating to the general drivers of the Royal Artillery, is to be understood as applying to the Waggon Train.

2. Lieutenant Steel, 48th regiment, is appointed to act as Adjutant to the 1st battalion of that regiment, till his Majesty's pleasure is known.

Adjutant

Adjutant Dixon, 48th regiment, is to do duty with the 2d battalion of that regiment.

ADJUTANT GENERAL's OFFICE.
Badajoz, 3d Dec. 1809.

G. O.

1. BRIGADIER General Cameron appointed, in the orders of 1st December, President of a General Court-Martial to assemble on the 4th instant, being from indisposition unequal to attend, that arrangement is cancelled; and Brigadier General Richard Stewart in succession is nominated President of the said General Court Martial.

2. Captain Francis Cockburne is appointed to execute the office of Judge Advocate, in the absence of the Deputy Judge Advocate of this army.

ADJUTANT GENERAL's OFFICE.
Badajoz, 5th Dec. 1809.

G. O.

2. The Commander of the Forces has read with much concern the report of the conduct of Lieutenant Ratcliffe of the 27th regiment, on the 25th of November, in the house in which he is quartered; and of Lieutenant Beaver, the Officer of the barrack guard of the 27th regiment, on the same day. The Officers quartered in Badajoz have been repeatedly informed, that if they have any occasion to complain of their landlords, they must make their complaints to Captain Kelly, of the Quarter-Master General's department, and by no means take into their own hands the redress of any supposed cause of complaint, which they may imagine they have against their landlords or other persons.

The

The conduct of Lieutenant Beaver the Officer of the Barrack Guard of the 27th regiment, in interfering with his guard between Lieutenant Ratcliffe and the Spanish guard, was still more improper than the conduct of Lieutenant Ratcliffe; and its indiscretion was equally manifested with its impropriety, as he was very shortly obliged to withdraw from all interference, by the superior numbers of the Spanish guard.

The Officers and troops in Badajoz are to understand that they are quartered in this town, only because it is a convenient station in the line of cantonments occupied by the army; but they are no part of the garrison of the fort, and have nothing to do with its duties.

The guards which are mounted by the British troops are solely for regimental or brigade purposes, and for the security of the stores of the army over which they are placed: they have nothing to say to the safety of the place or its police, as connected with its security.

The Commander of the Forces adopts this mode of expressing his disapprobation of the conduct of Lieutenants Ratcliffe and Beaver, of the 27th regiment. He desires however, that these Officers may be released from their arrest, as he hopes that what he has above stated will prevent them as well as others, from being guilty of such conduct in future.

ADJUTANT GENERAL'S OFFICE.

G. O.   *Badajoz, 7th Dec.* 1809.

Captain Hugonin, 4th Dragoons, is appointed to act as Brigade Major to Brigadier General Fane's brigade

of

of Heavy Dragoons, till the pleasure of his Majesty is known.

3. Mr. Deputy Commissary General Lutyens, Assistant Commissary Drake, Assistant Commissary Lukin, Acting Assistant Commissary Weekinges, Acting Assistant Commissary Percell, Acting Assistant Commissary Varnham, have arrived from England, and the following Officers of the Commissariat of this army have been promoted.

Acting Deputy Commissary General Boyce to be Deputy Commissary General.

Dep. Com. Gauntlett
———————— Aylmer } to be Acting Dep. Com. Gens.

Acting Asst. Com. Haines
———————— Downey } to be Assist. Commissaries
———————— Wemyss

Mr. William Fielder
——- Tupper Carey } to be Acting Asst. Commiss.

———

ADJUTANT GENERAL'S OFFICE.
Badajoz, 8th Dec. 1809.

G. O.

2. THE brigade of Guards, and the troops in Badajoz, are this day to receive from the Deputy Paymaster General, an advance equal to one third of their estimates to the 24th instant; the other corps in the 1st division will receive the same advance as they pass through Badajoz.

The regiments in the 2d and 3d divisions of Infantry will send for it to-morrow, and the 4th division and the Cavalry on the following day.

The Assistant Commissaries attached to brigades will inform the General Officers commanding brigades, of the

arrangements

arrangements made by the Commissary General for supplying the troops on the march, and the General Officers commanding divisions and brigades are requested to order the deliveries accordingly.

4. An additional number of blankets being arrived, the Officers commanding regiments are to make a requisition upon the Quarter-Master General for a sufficient number for one-fourth of their strength, which will complete the regiments to one blanket for each man. The Quarter-Master General will inform the different corps of the army in what manner they are to receive those allotted for them.

5. The Commander of the Forces requests that on the march which the army is about to make, the Officers will attend to the Orders of the 4th May, No. 5 and 6, and to the General Orders of the 7th October, No. 8, 9, 10, and 11, relating to the mode of making requisitions upon the country. In addition to these orders, the Commander of the Forces desires that when any Officer finds himself in the situation to be obliged to take articles of provisions or forage from the country upon his own receipts, he will report to his Commanding Officer that he has done so, specifying particularly the date, the place, and the articles for which he has given his receipt. The Commanding Officer will send this report to the Assistant Commissary attached to the brigade, regiment, or division, of the army to which the Officer belongs.

G. A. O.

ADJUTANT GENERAL'S OFFICE.
Badajoz, 9th Dec. 1809.

COMMANDING Officers of regiments in want of shoes are requested to apply to the Quarter-Master General, who will let them know how they can be supplied.

G. A. O.

ADJUTANT GENERAL'S OFFICE.
Badajoz, 10*th Dec.* 1809.

LIEUTENANT James Shaw, of the 43d Regiment, is appointed Aide-de-Camp to Brigadier General Robert Crawford, bearing date from the 19th November last.

G.·O.

ADJUTANT GENERAL'S OFFICE.
Badajoz, 11*th Dec.* 1809.

Memorandum.—THE Commander of the Forces has been pleased to make the following appointments, bearing date from the 15th November last, till his Majesty's pleasure is known:

Surgeon Backmeister, 66th Regiment, to be Surgeon to the Forces.

Surgeon Guthrie, 29th Regiment, to be Surgeon to the Forces.

Surgeon Von Millenger, from the 60th Regiment, to be Surgeon to the 31st Regiment, vice M'Gilloray, deceased.

Assistant Surgeon Stanford, from the 3d Regiment,

(or

(or Buffs,) to be Surgeon to the 29th Regiment, vice Guthrie, promoted.

Assistant Surgeon Wardall, 57th Regiment, to be Surgeon to the 66th Regiment, vice Backmeister, promoted.

Assistant Surgeon Moore, 82d Regiment, to be Surgeon to the 60th, vice Von Millenger, promoted to the 31st Regiment.

Hospital Mate Frederick Browne to be Assistant Surgeon to the 3d, (or Buffs,) vice Stanford, promoted.

Hospital Mate Christopher Humphrey to be Assistant Surgeon to the 57th Regiment, vice Wardall, promoted.

Hospital Mate George Lardner to be Assistant Surgeon to the 14th Light Dragoons, vice M'Gilloray, promoted.

Hospital Mate George Hilson to be Assistant Surgeon to the 24th Foot.

Hospital Mate Henry Snow to be Assistant Surgeon to the 57th Regiment.

Hospital Mate Thomas Fidden to be Assistant Surgeon to the 9th Foot, vice Milne, deceased.

Hospital Mate William Moffatt to be Assistant Surgeon to the 48th Regiment, 2d battalion.

Hospital Mate William Sander to be Assistant Surgeon to the 4th Dragoons, vice Moore, promoted.

Acting Deputy Purveyor Henry Bacon to be Deputy Purveyor to the Forces, vice Maypother, promoted.

Acting Deputy Purveyor John Winter to be Deputy Purveyor to the Forces.

Assistant Commissary Haydon is attached to and will do duty with Major General Cole's brigade, vice Mr. Assistant Commissary Nelson transferred to Colonel Kemmis's brigade.

G. O.

ADJUTANT GENERAL'S OFFICE.
Badajoz, 12th Dec. 1809.

G. O.

SERJEANT Major Hugh Fleming, 3d Foot Guards, is appointed to act as Adjutant to the 2d battalion 24th Regiment till his Majesty's pleasure is known.

ADJUTANT GENERAL'S OFFICE.
Badajoz, 13th Dec. 1809.

A. G. O.

1. THE Commander of the Forces is concerned to notice the continued and repeated disobedience of Orders by the Officers of the army, in pressing mules and carts, and in taking articles from the country upon their own informal receipts. He is concerned to be obliged to resort to measures to enforce obedience to his orders, and he now directs that Captain Parsons, of the 48th Regiment, may be put in arrest by the Commanding Officer of the Hospital, at Elvas, for taking away mules belonging to the Commissariat, at Badajoz, contrary to orders; his crime will be sent to him by the Adjutant General, and he is to proceed forthwith to Badajoz.

2. The Commander of the Forces calls the attention of the Officers of the army to the following order, by the late Commander of the Forces, in Portugal.

Extract from General Orders, by Lieutenant General Sir John Craddock.

No. 2. " The army is referred to the Orders of the 14th March, on the subject of quarters, which General Officers

Officers are requested to impress on the troops under their command; and it is to be clearly understood that cover is all that any Officer has a right to expect, and he has no. pretensions to ask for either bed or furniture; when such articles are supplied, it is a matter of civility on the part of the owner, and must be received as a favour, and not as a right."

This principle has been before laid down in General Orders, and must be extended throughout this kingdom.

ADJUTANT GENERAL'S OFFICE.

Badajoz, 14th Dec. 1809.

G. A. O.

THE General Court Martial, of which Brigadier General R. Stewart is President, is adjourned, and the Officers composing it are to return to duty in their respective regiments.

The Commander of the Forces is happy to find that the circumstances respecting the conduct of Captain Parsons, 48th Regiment, did not occur as they were represented to him by the Officer of the Commissariat department, Mr. Daulmery, and that he is therefore enabled to release that Officer from his arrest, notwithstanding that an irregularity was committed by the soldiers under his command.

Captain Parsons is therefore released from his arrest, and is to join his regiment.

G. O.

ADJUTANT GENERAL's OFFICE.

G. O. Badajoz, 15th Dec. 1809.

Memorandum.—THE Commander of the Forces has been pleased to make the following appointments until his Majesty's pleasure is known, bearing date, Badajoz, 14th December, 1809.

Surgeon Richard Beachall, 97th Regiment, to be Surgeon to the Forces, vice Lindsay, promoted.

Assistant Surgeon M'Kenzie, 1st or Royal Dragoons, to be Surgeon to the 39th Regiment, vice Kidd, deceased.

Assistant Surgeon J. Dumoulin, 5th battalion 60th Regiment, to be Surgeon to the 97th, vice Beachall, promoted.

Hospital Mate William Langham to be Assistant Surgeon to the 1st or Royal Dragoons, vice M'Kenzie, promoted.

Hospital Mate David Pearston to be Assistant Surgeon to the 60th Regiment, vice Dumoulin, promoted.

Mr. D. Barry to be Assistant Surgeon to the 2d battalion 58th Regiment.

ADJUTANT GENERAL's OFFICE.

G. O. Badajoz, 16th Dec. 1809.

SERJEANT Major Thomas Fanning, of the 3d battalion 27th Foot, is appointed an Assistant Provost, and he is to do duty with the 4th division of Infantry; the horse belonging to the late Assistant Provost Pillan is to be handed over to the Assistant Provost Fanning.

Serjeant

Serjeant Major Davies, of the 3d Regiment, (or Buffs,) is appointed an Assistant Provost Marshal, and is to do duty at Lisbon.

Mr. Le Court is to act as a Staff Surgeon with the army, and is to receive pay and allowances accordingly, from the 25th November.

Mr. Le Court, jun. is to act as an Hospital Mate with the army, and is to receive pay and allowances accordingly, from 25th November.

ADJUTANT GENERAL'S OFFICE.
Badajoz, 17th Dec. 1809.

G. O.

1. THE Officer commanding the General Hospitals, at Elvas, Estremoz, and Villa Viciosa, is to appoint a Board of Officers at each of those places to examine the arms, accoutrements, clothing, &c. belonging to soldiers now in hospital, or who have been discharged from the hospital, or have died, which articles may be in the possession of the Purveyor General at the present moment.

This Board is to make a register of these articles by regiments, inserting in the register the marks or names on each article.

Of this register one copy must be given to the Purveyor General, and one copy forwarded to the Adjutant General's Office, to be communicated to the several regiments.

2. The Assistant Quarter-Master General, at Elvas, must be one of the members of this Board.

3. The Purveyor General must be particularly careful in keeping the register of arms, &c. brought by the sol-

R 4

diers.

diers to the General Hospital in future, in obedience to his Majesty's regulations of the 31st of March, 1800.

4. In order to enable the Purveyor General, or his Deputy, to obey this order, the Officers commanding regiments are invariably to send with a soldier to the hospital, whether general, brigade, detachment, or regimental, a Ticket make out in the following form:

To the Purveyor of his Majesty's Hospital at

SIR,

Please to receive into the Hospital the following Men of the   dated   the day of   18

<table>
<tr><td rowspan="8">FRONT.</td><td>Men's Names.</td><td>Troop or Company.</td><td>Disease, and how long Ill.</td><td>N. B. This must be signed by one Commanding Officer, besides the Surgeon or his Mate, as underneath.</td></tr>
<tr><td></td><td></td><td></td><td>Captain ———</td></tr>
<tr><td></td><td></td><td></td><td>Lieut. ———</td></tr>
<tr><td></td><td></td><td></td><td>Cornet ———</td></tr>
<tr><td></td><td></td><td></td><td>Ensign ———</td></tr>
<tr><td></td><td></td><td></td><td>Surgeon ———</td></tr>
<tr><td></td><td></td><td></td><td>Surg. Mate ———</td></tr>
</table>

Return

Return of Arms, Accoutrements, and Necessaries, sent with him.

REAR.

Men's Names.	Troop or Company.	Necessaries.										Clothing.					Arms and Accoutrements.									
		Shirts.	Shoes.	Stockings.	Brushes.	Black Balls.	Combs.	Great Coat Straps.	Stock and Clasp.	Gaiters.	Knapsack.	Cap and Tuft.	Coat.	Waistcoat.	Breeches.	Great Coat.	Fusil or Halbert.	No. or Mark on ditto.	Musquet.	No. or Mark on ditto.	Bayonet and Scabbard.	Sling.	Bayonet Belt.	Pouch Belt, and Pouch.	Haversack.	Canteen and Strap.
	TOTAL																									

5. When men are sent to a general or detachment hospital by any regiment, the Officer commanding must report to the General Officer commanding the brigade whether this order has been obeyed.

6. The Purveyor General, or the Medical Officer, in charge of the arms, accoutrements, &c. in any hospital, must report immediately any instance in which obedience to this order may have been neglected, otherwise he will be considered responsible for all loss and damage of arms and accoutrements of soldiers in hospital.

7. The Officer commanding at Lisbon will give directions that these orders, respecting the formation of the registry, &c. may be carried into execution at the General Hospital at Lisbon.

———

ADJUTANT GENERAL'S OFFICE.

G. O.   *Badajoz, 18th Dec. 1809.*

1. In order to prevent the inconvenience which the army would suffer from the absence of the Officers of the Staff, the Commander of the Forces has determined that all Officers belonging to the departments of the Adjutant and Quarter-Master General of the army in Spain and Portugal, who shall be absent from the Peninsula, on any account, except that of having been wounded, shall cease to receive their Staff pay and allowances in two months from the period of their embarkation, although they will continue on the list of their respective departments, and will return to their duties in them, when they will rejoin the army.

The Adjutant and Quarter-Master General will attend

to

to this order in making up the abstracts of their several departments.

2. Major Brooke, of the 5th Regiment, is appointed to act as an Assistant in the Quarter-Master General's department till his Majesty's pleasure is known.

ADJUTANT GENERAL'S OFFICE.

G. O.   *Badajoz, 19th Dec. 1809.*

(Copy.)   HORSE GUARDS.
                              23d Nov. 1809.

MY LORD,

1. HAVING laid before the King the proceedings of a General Court Martial held at Lisbon on the 10th October, 1809, and continued by adjournment to the 12th of the same month for the trial of Hospital Mate George Welsh, who was arraigned upon the undermentioned charges, viz.

1st. For having drawn at different times a sword belonging to a private of the 14th Light Dragoons, running through the hospital, and bringing in this manner the sick to bed.

2d. Making use of very improper language to Captain Plate, Independent Garrison Company King's German Legion, when inspecting the hospital at Santarem, as Senior Officer, on the evening of the 4th of August.

3d. Disobeying the orders, as well of Staff Surgeon Dr. Heine and of Captain Plate, on the 5th, 6th, and 7th

of

of August, and behaving, particularly on the 5th, in a very ungentlemanlike manner.

4th. Neglecting his duty at different times, leaving the sick for many days without any physic, but particularly on the 23d of August, when he moved with the hospital to Lisbon, and left nine sick men behind without informing the Commanding Officer or a Portuguese Medical Officer of it.

Upon which charges the Court came to the following decision:

The Court having duly weighed the evidence adduced on the part of the prosecution, together with what the prisoner, Hospital Mate Doctor Welsh, has urged in his defence, is of opinion that he is guilty of having once drawn a sword belonging to a private of the 14th Light Dragoons, running through the hospital, and bringing in this manner the sick to bed. The Court is of opinion that the prisoner, Hospital Mate Dr. Welsh, is guilty of the 2d charge.

With respect to the 3d charge, the Court is of opinion that the prisoner, Hospital Mate Dr. Welsh, is guilty of disobeying the orders of Staff Surgeon Dr. Heine, but acquit him of the remainder of the charge. With respect to the 4th charge, no evidence being brought forward, they acquit him thereof; and upon the whole the Court doth adjudge that Hospital Mate Dr. Welsh be dismissed his Majesty's service.

I am to acquaint your Lordship that his Majesty has been pleased to approve of the finding and sentence of the Court. Your Lordship will therefore acquaint me with the day upon which the sentence is made known to the

prisoner,

prisoner, Hospital Mate George Welsh, as from that day he will cease to receive pay in his Majesty's service.

(Signed)   D. DUNDAS.
Commander in Chief.

To Lieut. General Rt. Hon.
Lord Visc. Wellington, K. B.
&c.   &c.   &c.

2. Mr. James Morley is to act as Staff Surgeon with the army, and is to receive pay and allowances accordingly, from 25th November.

G. O.   ADJUTANT GENERAL'S OFFICE.
Badajoz, 23d Dec. 1809.

3. BADAJOZ, December 9th, 1809.—The Court, of which Brigadier General Richard Stewart was President, having re-assembled, proceeded to the trial of Assistant Surgeon Hickson, 4th Dragoons, arraigned on the following charges:

1st. For quitting Talavera de Le Reyna on or about the morning of the 4th of August last without leave, and proceeding to join his regiment near Oropesa, he having been directed to remain at the former place with the sick and wounded, in conformity to the General Orders of the 2d of the same month.

2d. For absenting himself from his regiment without leave of his Commanding Officer, on or about the 5th of August last, and not returning to his duty till on or about the 14th of the same month.

To which charges, the prisoner, Assistant Surgeon
Hickson,

Hickson, 4th Dragoons, pleaded not guilty, and the Court proceeded to the examination of evidence.

OPINION AND SENTENCE.

The Court having maturely and deliberately weighed and considered the evidence produced in support of the charges preferred against the prisoner, Assistant Surgeon Hickson, 4th Dragoons, as well as that which he has produced in his defence, are of opinion that he (the prisoner) is guilty of the charges preferred against him, viz. For quitting Talavera de La Reyna, on or about the morning of the 4th of August last, without leave, and proceeding to join his regiment near Oropesa, he having been directed to remain at the former place with the sick and wounded, in conformity to the General Orders of the 2d of the same month.

2d. For absenting himself from his regiment without leave of his Commanding Officer, on or about the 5th of August last, and not returning to his duty till on or about the 14th of the same month, being in breach of the Articles of War, and do by virtue thereof sentence him, the prisoner, Assistant Surgeon Hickson, 4th Dragoons, to be suspended from rank and pay for the space of six calendar months.

The Court are induced to award this sentence from the circumstance of the prisoner having, by an accident, been in a great measure unfitted for the duties of his station, and from his having quitted Talavera with the knowledge of Mr. Staff Surgeon Cooke, under whose immediate orders he had previously acted.

This decision has been confirmed by his Excellency: in consequence, however, of the recommendation of the
General

General Court Martial, the Commander of the Forces is induced to pardon Assistant Surgeon Hickson.

That Officer is to be released from his arrest, and is to join his regiment.

G. O.

ADJUTANT GENERAL'S OFFICE.
Badajoz, 24th Dec. 1809.

Memorandum.—THE reserve of Royal Artillery, the Royal Staff Corps, 27th Regiment, and detachments ordered to march on Monday the 25th instant, will move in corps under the direction of the Senior Officer, who will take the previous instructions of Brigadier General Howarth.

Lieutenant Colonel Robe will take all measures to ensure the timely supply, regular march, and quartering of the troops, for which he is to be responsible.

G. O.

ADJUTANT GENERAL'S OFFICE.
Gavion, 28th Dec. 1809.

THE Commander of the Forces requests the Officers commanding divisions will direct the Officers of the Quarter-Master General's department attached to them respectively to arrange with the Magistrates of the different towns and villages in which the troops may be cantoned, in what houses General Officers, Field Officers, Captains, and Subalterns, respectively, shall be quartered; and the Officers are to be quartered according to this arrangement

The

The Commander of the Forces is concerned to notice that complaints of the conduct of some of the Officers of the army to the inhabitants of Portugal have already reached him, and he is convinced that it must be of those who have lately joined the army, and were not partakers of the kindness with which the whole army were treated by the people this of country at the commencement of the campaign.

There is no doubt that by civility and good treatment the Officers of the army will receive from the inhabitants of Portugal again all the assistance and kindness which they can afford, and the Commander of the Forces is exceedingly anxious that the people of this country should not be brought by the misconduct of the army to detest those who are sent here to assist them in the defence of their country.

He particularly desires that the Officers on the Commissariat and Medical Staff will pay attention to these orders, and that the Commissary General will send a copy of them to each of the Commissaries who are detached.

END OF VOL. I.

INDEX.

INDEX.

VOL. I.

———

s 2

Ensign

s 3   The

No

The

General

Captain

The

Paymaster

To

The

Brigadier

Surgeon

Appointment

Sentence

Appointment